Bruce Cole

THE POP COMPOSER'S HANDBOOK

A step-by-step guide to the composition of melody, harmony, rhythm and structure

Styles and song-writing techniques from Rock, Reggae and Salsa to Bhangra, Club and Steel Band

U.C.B.
LIBRARY

www.schott-music.com

BARNS

D1471126

SCHOTT

ɴ York · Paris · Prague · Tokyo · Toronto
6 SCHOTT MUSIC Ltd., London · Printed in Germany

3000326b

For Maggie

The author and publisher would like to thank Peter Nickol and Paul Terry for their invaluable assistance in preparing this project for publication.

The publisher would also like to thank the following for allowing the use of their copyright material in this book:

The Music Sales Group and The Burt F. Bacharach Trust (*Close to You*, p. 91)
(They Long To Be) Close To You: Words by Hal David, Music by Burt Bacharach
© Copyright 1963 Casa David Music Incorporated/New Hidden Valley Music Company, USA
Copyright Renewed © 1991 New Hidden Valley Music and Casa David
Windswept Music (London) Limited (50%)/Universal/MCA Music Limited (50%).
All Rights Reserved. International Copyright Secured.
Used by permission of Music Sales Limited.

EMI Music Publishing Limited (*My Cherie Amour*, p. 95)
My Cherie Amour: Words and Music by Stevie Wonder, Sylvia Moy and Henry Cosby
© 1968, Jobete Music Co Inc/ Black Bull Music Inc/Stone Agate Music/ Sawandi Music, USA
Reproduced by permission of Black Bull Music Inc/Jobete Music Co, London WC2H 0QY.

British Library Cataloguing-in-Publication Data.
A catalogue record of this book is available from the British Library.

ED 12723
ISBN 1–902455–60–6
ISMN M–2201–2192–0

© 2006 Schott Music Ltd, London. All rights reserved. Printed in Germany.
No part of this publication may be reproduced, stored in a retrieval system, or transmitted, in any form or by any means, electronic, mechanical, photocopying, recording or otherwise, without the prior written permission of Schott Music Ltd, 48 Great Marlborough Street, London WlF 7BB

Designed and typeset by Peter Nickol
Cover design: H.-J. Kropp
Printed in Germany

Contents

PART 2 – TOPICS

PART 3 – PROJECT PLANNING

Preface

It would have been ideal if this handbook could have been published with a CD of examples. However, it would have made the book prohibitively expensive – a mere glance at the list of artists and songs in the index will indicate how long it might have taken to clear all the copyrights. In the end, I made the decision to base the examples on readily available recordings. All the songs mentioned should be in someone's collection – if not the teacher or a student, then perhaps a student's parents. In any case, the songs are all well known and will be available in a 'best of' or 'greatest hits' collection.

The book is divided into three sections. The first chapters are linked, forming a progression, but can also be regarded as free-standing, to be taken in any order or 'dipped into'. The second section covers a range of styles and topics, and the third is of more general interest, covering whole-class projects, the design of worksheets, and schemes of work which link together and draw on the projects, exercises and lesson plans found elsewhere in the book.

Practical work is identified according to its anticipated difficulty, on a scale of four quavers. (One quaver = easy; four quavers = most challenging.) Obviously some of these ability ranges will overlap, and I have not made any attempt to grade the more advanced student who will probably be working alone and can draw on any of the projects for an individual assignment or work plan.

There are many chord charts. These are all in easy keys – even if that meant transposing relative to the original recording. Occasionally, in order to make a point, I have referred to chords by their Roman numerals, but overall I have tried to avoid the technicalities of music theory. Most popular musicians manage without – even those who enter the music industry with a classical background. Teachers who know their students well will know how and when it is appropriate to explain technical matters.

CHAPTER 1

Rhythm

For related sections see Riffs (page 79), Latino (page 103), Samba (page 128).

Introduction

Of all the musical elements, rhythm is perhaps the most important in popular music. It gives character to the melody and harmony. It defines the style, and the **rhythm section** of percussion and bass instruments acts as the 'engine' of the band, driving the music forwards and articulating its structure.

INTRODUCTORY ACTIVITIES ♪

Exercise 1

This is for anyone claiming not to have a sense of rhythm. Mark time by marching on the spot: left, right, left, right. This will establish a beat.

Now count out loud in time with the marching footsteps:
    left   right left   right,
    one   two   three four
Now clap on two and four.

You have now established the notion of the **backbeat**, a fundamental feature of popular rhythm: a strong beat followed by a weak beat with a stress on the weak one.

Development

Clap the backbeat to a recording of Queen's *We Will Rock You*. Note the heavy bass drum, the handclap and the slow-slow-quick-quick-slow pattern.

Exercise 2

This is a listening exercise. Compare recordings of two performances: Tchaikovsky's *The Nutcracker* or Grieg's *Peer Gynt Suite* with Duke Ellington's arrangements of the same pieces. Discuss the principal differences. Ellington adopts a **swing** rhythm (compound rather than simple time – but see page 12 for a more detailed explanation of swing); his melodies are more **syncopated** (many of the original melody notes are anticipated, or 'pushed'); and a drum part is added.

Key features of rhythm in popular music

➤ a backbeat

➤ a drum kit (or other percussion)

➤ a recognisable repeated pattern that gives the music its *feel*

➤ syncopation

GAMES AND WARM-UPS ♪

Table-top drumming

> **To the teacher**
>
> This is for the whole class. It can be performed with each member standing behind his or her desk holding drum sticks and using the desk top as a drum (if no drum sticks are available then tapped pencils or handclapping will do).
>
> What is more interesting and enjoyable is to form a circle, each class member having an upturned chair in front of them, to be played like a drum kit with the seat as a snare drum and the legs as cymbals. However, this may prove too impractical for some classrooms, so desks or tables may have to do.

First, establish a pulse. The teacher beats four straight crotchets and the class answers:

Next, the teacher improvises a one-bar pattern and the class copies:

Now use this principle to perform an eight-bar exercise in which everyone will eventually have a chance to improvise three bars.

To establish an example, the teacher starts with four straight crotchets, played on the table top and answered by the whole class. Then the teacher improvises a bar of rhythm, also copied by the whole class; then another bar, and then another, resulting in eight bars in all. Here is an example written out:

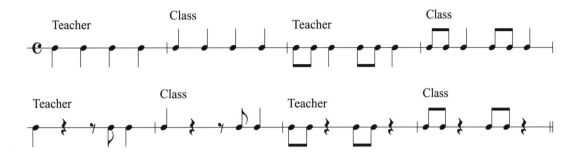

Having completed the eight bars, the leadership passes to a member of the class – who begins with four straight crotchets, like the teacher. After completing these eight bars another member of the class takes over until everyone has had a go. The eight-bar cycles should follow each other without a break, so the pulse is maintained.

You will find that it gets harder if you introduce rests.

Football rhythm

Everyone knows the football terrace handclap:

This is an exercise intended to develop concentration on the pulse. Start with the teacher clapping the two-bar pattern, answered by the class. This will tighten up the clapping ensemble and establish a tempo. Now divide the class into two. The first group starts and the second group follows at two crotchets' distance.

Now divide the class into four: the four groups enter, one by one, at two crotchets' distance as above. You can also try accenting some of the beats.

Clave

Clave is the basic rhythm of Latin music, pronounced 'clarvay'. (See Chapters 9 and 11.) It is best led by the teacher, call-and-response style.

This exercise builds up the pattern in stages so as to demonstrate the principle of syncopation. We start by clapping a simple unsyncopated rhythm:

Now place the second clap ahead of the beat – a classic rhythmic device in popular music:

Introduce a rest at the start of bar 2 (it may help if you foot-tap where the clap used to be):

For extra subtlety, delay the last note:

Style, metre and tempo

Rhythm is an important feature in determining style in popular music, whether rock, dance or reggae, and very often this boils down to the drum pattern – a basic repeated unit, one bar long and consisting essentially of a three-part texture of bass drum, snare drum and cymbal (usually the hi-hat cymbal). On a drum machine or electronic keyboard, a hundred or more drum patterns may be available, all categorised according to style: rock, pop, disco, funk, reggae, or a variety of Latin patterns (samba, rumba, tango, etc.).

Rock patterns

These tend to be a simple four-in-a-bar. The backbeat is played on the snare, and the hi-hat is played in eights (quavers) or fours (crotchets). The bass drum parts have the most variety, sometimes even within a song. Here are some examples:

hi-hat
snare drum
bass drum

The backbeat is not always exactly on the offbeat:

In some styles it is the hi-hat patterning that is characteristic. Disco tends to employ sixteens (semiquavers) on a closed hi-hat, although the basic pattern is a rock one (this pattern will also fit the many Latin styles). The drummer uses both sticks on the hi-hat, striking the snare on the second and fourth beats:

The hi-hat can be lifted with a foot pedal to create a splash. Some disco patterns make a feature of this with a splash on each offbeat quaver:

Philadelphia soul gives a characteristic lift on the last hi-hat quaver:

Club dance (see Chapter 10 for more details) employs more complex patterns of hi-hat lifts over a steady pulsing bass drum:

Shuffle and swing

The classic rock'n'roll shuffle pattern is created by playing a dotted rhythm on the hi-hat:

The swing feel, common in jazz, is similar, but with a more lazy triplet pattern. It often has only one backbeat, giving it a 'half time' feel. The cymbal part is usually played on the ride cymbal rather than the hi-hat. The snare drum is played with brushes (a technique which drum machines do not imitate well):

A blues shuffle – as used, for example, by Howling Wolf or John Lee Hooker (and later by bands such as the Rolling Stones) – has a more continuous driving triplet pattern:

Before ending this section, a quick word about tempo (sometimes referred to as BPM – beats per minute). Choosing the right tempo is often crucial to the success of a performance. A song played too slow or too fast will sound 'wrong'.

ACTIVITIES ♪

Building a three-part drum pattern

This activity can be undertaken by groups of three (or possibly pairs) playing percussion instruments, electronic keyboards with percussion sounds, vocalising or inventing body percussion.

Each member of the group takes one of the three basic drum parts: bass, snare and hi-hat. The task is to devise a one-bar pattern, fit it together and perform it as a repeated pattern.

When the groups play their patterns, see if the class can guess the style.

This activity can form the starting point for the next one, and also for the lesson plan below, 'Constructing a Drum Track'.

Variations

Working in the same size groups, take the one-bar pattern from the activity above (or invent a new one) and compose a set of variations on it. It may be helpful to work to a structural guideline, for example: 'Each pattern must be repeated four times before the next variation'.

Variations might take the following forms:

➤ Varying the bass, snare and hi-hat parts

➤ Playing the pattern in different styles

➤ Adding a second bar to make a two-bar pattern

➤ Changing the metre (e.g. from 4/4 to 3/4)

Building on a one-bar pattern

Few song arrangements consist of a one-bar drum pattern played over and over. Usually the drums follow the melody or chord changes, signposting structural features like choruses and middles with **fills** and **punctuation**.

A fill is a short improvised pattern, and is used to mark the end of a section or phrase and the start of another. It can be played on the tom-toms and cymbals, or it can be a simple pattern on the snare.

Punctuation is a technique employed by a drummer to accentuate features of the song – a crucial word in the lyrics, a particular chord or a rhythmic pattern in a guitar part. It can take the form of a change of accent or a cymbal crash.

Also, a band may include a percussionist as well as a drummer, playing a range of cymbals, congas and even tuned percussion to add rhythmic interest (see Chapter 5).

The amount of complexity added by a drummer varies from band to band. The drumming of Keith Moon of the Who was often like a solo part in its own right (listen to his drumming on *Quadrophenia*), whilst the drumming in contemporary rock bands is often much simpler (e.g. Franz Ferdinand). The electronic drum parts of 1980s electro rock are simpler still, almost robotic (e.g. Ultravox, Human League, Orchestral Manoeuvres in the Dark).

In building a drum track, the most simple, basic structure is the four- or eight-bar phrase – a pattern played three (or seven) times with a decorative fill in the last bar:

Constructing a drum track

Equipment

The objective is to compose and perform a drum track. This can be played by a small group using keyboard percussion or hand-held percussion; or it can be entered onto a computer (see below) by students working in pairs; or it can be played by a kit drummer working alone.

Preparatory work

You should have completed the activity on page 13.

Task

Build a 16-bar drum track as follows:

Bars 1–4	Devise a pattern to use in the first three bars, and with a fill in the fourth.
Bars 5–8	A variant of the first pattern, with a fill in the eighth bar.
Bars 9–16	A new pattern, with a 'roll-out' in the 16th bar. This is a short fill or flourish.
Bar 17	The preceding roll-out is finished off on the first beat of the next bar. It can be 'dry' (without a cymbal splash) or 'wet' (with a cymbal).

Development

Play bars 1–16 and then repeat bars 1–8 to create a simple ABA structure. You will have to play a fill in bar 16 (because it now leads to a repeat) and place the roll-out and final note in the last two bars.

Using technology

MIDI and sampled percussion

Many percussion tracks are a mixture of samples and MIDI sounds. There are more details about music technology in Chapters 5 and 10, but for now we should clarify that samples are short audio recordings; they are imported into an audio track on your sequencing program, usually loaded from a CD of samples. MIDI sounds are contained in your computer's sound card, and must be entered either with a MIDI keyboard or by using the mouse to enter notes one at a time on an editing display.

MIDI patterns can be compiled using drum editors – most programs have one. The sounds are listed on the left, and the grid is divided into sixteen squares (four beats each subdivided into four). You enter a drum sound by cross-matching a beat with a sound and clicking in the box.

BEAT	I			2			3			4			
Bass drum	x						x		x				
Snare drum				x						x			
Hi-hat closed	x	x	x		x	x	x	x	x	x			x	x
Hi-hat open				x			x			x				x
Handclap													x	x
Crash cymbal											x			

An advantage of working on a computer is that it can play patterns which a live player would find impossible. This feature is exploited by composers of club music who typically write hi-hat patterns with a complex combination of closed sounds and lifts.

Some programs, like Fruity Loops or Reason, will allow you to compile a drum pattern by entering individual sampled drum sounds. The program itself will include some samples, but you can also load them from a CD. The drum pattern is compiled in exactly the same way as on a MIDI drum editor.

Feel and groove

Although the examples of drum patterns in this chapter have been written out in notation, the differences between regular and syncopated rhythms, or between dotted rhythms and triplets, are not straightforward in popular music. Actually there are many subtleties – musicians will often play a rhythm somewhere in between the notated values, the entire band bonding together to create a **groove** which is impossible to notate precisely. Reproducing a groove using a computer programme is discussed on the next two pages.

Play a recording of swing jazz (e.g. by Glenn Miller) and compare it with an example of ska, the forerunner of Jamaican reggae (compilation CDs are available). Strictly speaking, both are in compound quadruple time – 12/8 – yet the rhythm of the triplet patterns is quite different: the swing jazz pattern is lazier, more like a dotted quaver and semiquaver, whilst the ska pattern is more triplet-like, with the off-beat quaver fractionally early.

Another example of a groove occurs in funk, where the rhythmic patterns are heavily syncopated and consist of a complex marriage of parts. An example of a heavy funk backing occurs in the Red Hot Chilli Peppers' *Give it Away*. Another band that specialises in funk grooves is Jamiroquai.

Establishing a tight groove is one of the great arts of band musicianship. But although a groove may be too subtle to be notated accurately in a score, it is possible to create a groove on a computer using a sequencing program. Typically, the program divides the bar into 'ticks'. In Cubase, for example, a crotchet beat lasts 384 ticks. It is therefore possible to work out rhythms numerically, with great accuracy.

Sequencing programs display the pitches and rhythms on an event editor (sometimes called a list editor). The editor shows the position of a note as a set of numbers down to the last tick, for example:

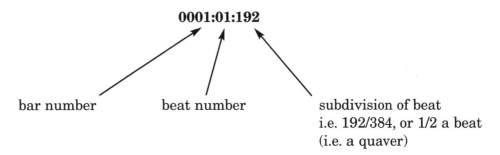

You can use the editor to move any note in the bar simply by clicking with the mouse on the numbers.

Important: if you reduce a number you will make the note play earlier, and if you add to it you will make it play later.

This technique allows you to make very fine adjustments to the rhythmic feel – an adjustment of one tick out of 384 will be imperceptible. The range of possibilities is illustrated on the next page.

Look at the diagram below. It illustrates four ways of numerically codifying a swing/shuffle rhythm, showing the values in ticks. The event editor gives us an unbroken range of 144 ticks from straight quavers at position 192 through to double dotted quavers at position 48.

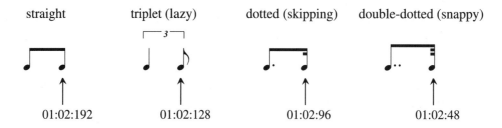

straight	triplet (lazy)	dotted (skipping)	double-dotted (snappy)
01:02:192	01:02:128	01:02:96	01:02:48

Composers and producers use this technique to add interest to drum patterns (and to the rhythm of other instrumental parts as well). If you compile a MIDI drum pattern using an editor as shown in the chart on page 16, the computer will almost certainly place every sound exactly on the beat, and this may give the pattern a mechanical feel you do not want.

It is quite common, for example, to make the backbeat of a rock drum pattern play fractionally ahead of the beat (which tends to drive the music forwards) or behind the beat (which creates tension). Try experimenting with a simple one-bar pattern. Some programs will allow you to make adjustments while they are running, so you can hear the changes as you go along; in others, you have to make the change and then play the pattern. Also, avoid the temptation to overdo it – a note which is moved too far out of line will make the rhythm feel uneasy, and too many notes pulled out of line will make the whole thing sound messy. Also, bear in mind that the drum pattern will eventually have to fit with other instruments. A good groove is one in which they all adopt the same subtleties.

Lastly, remember that when you move a note back, it is sometimes then displayed as part of the beat *before*. This can be confusing when the display suddenly changes, but rely on your ears – does it sound right?

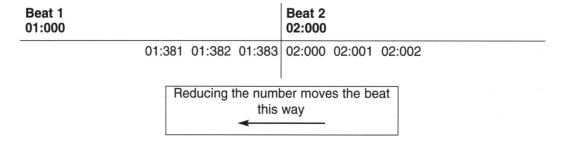

Working with samples

A lot of contemporary popular music is composed using samples: short, digital recordings of drum patterns, bass lines, etc., that can be imported into a studio program like Cubase, Logic or Audition and assembled into a composition. The problem with samples is that, because they come from different sources, they are not all the same length, nor at the same tempo, so if you want to combine them you have to make adjustments. This process is called 'time stretching' and allows you to change the tempo or transpose the key. The process is explained in Chapter 10.

The next chapter opens with ideas about linking rhythm with melody.

CHAPTER 2

Melody

If rhythm is the element that drives the music forwards and makes us want to dance, then the melody is the feature that we all remember and go away singing. There is a strong relationship between rhythm and melody, and one important linking factor is the lyrics and the way they are set. We might think of melody writing as a creative triangle:

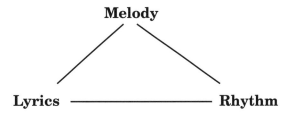

Lyric writing is a craft in its own right. Some songwriters compose both the music and the lyrics – Sting, for example – whilst others compose the music to someone else's lyrics – for example Elton John and his lyricist Bernie Taupin. There is not space in this book to cover lyric writing in detail, but a study of pop melody will be easier if we first look briefly at the relationship between words and music:

➤ Most pop melodies involve a **syllabic** setting of the words – that is, there is usually one melody note per syllable. Some singers like to embellish the end of a phrase with a short **melisma** or vocal run, sung to a single syllable. Examples of longer melismas occur in the singing of soul divas like Whitney Houston, Mariah Carey and Christina Aguilera, who employ vocal gymnastics to extend a whole phrase. Melismas are common in classical music, particularly opera.

➤ Some lyrics are in a clear metre – for example *Mull of Kintyre* (Paul McCartney) in 3/4, or *Benny and the Jets* (Elton John) in 4/4. Both melodies closely follow the implied rhythm of the words. Other lyrics are less obviously metrical. Those of Morrissey, for example, give little clue to the rhythm, and are more like **blank verse**.

➤ Many lyrics contain an **anacrusis** – starting with a weak word leading into a stronger one. Musically this becomes an **upbeat** – a weak beat (usually the last beat of one bar) leading into a strong beat (the first beat of the next bar). A good example is *Auld Lang Syne*: 'Should <u>auld</u> acquaintance be forgot...'. Upbeats can cause counting problems with inexperienced or untrained musicians.

➤ The rhyming structure of the lyrics can have a significant effect on the structure of the melodic phrases. Many lines of verse are grouped in fours (one of the reasons why the four-bar chord pattern has developed as such a strong feature of popular music – see Chapter 3). Some common patterns are:

AABB e.g. cloud, crowd, free, see
ABAB e.g. run, away, fun, day
ABCB e.g. work, game, people, same

It is quite common for the melodic phrases to follow the rhyming structure. For instance, an AABB rhyme might be set to two melodic phrases – melody A (repeated) followed by melody B (repeated):

Stand-ing here be-neath a cloud, Al-ways with a big-ger crowd.

Don't know why I feel so free, No-thing here for me to see.

EXERCISES ♪

The following exercises form an introduction to the art of word setting.

Putting in accents

Using an anthology, copy out a verse from a rhyming poem. Try reciting the poem and mark the words where the accents go. Those with a knowledge of music theory can try putting in bar lines.

In **spring**, when **woods** are **get**ting **green**,

I'll **try** and **tell** you **what** I **mean**.

In **sum**mer, **when** the **days** are **long**

Per**haps** you'll **under**stand the **song**.

from *Humpty Dumpty's Song* by Lewis Carroll

Cut outs

For this activity – which will work for individuals, pairs or groups – you will need a pile of comics, magazines, or poems plus a sheet of A4 paper, scissors and a glue stick.

Search for words, phrases or slogans, cutting out those you think may fit into a clearly defined metre. Arrange them on the A4 sheet to make a set of lyrics and try chanting them. The easiest way is for each member of the group to take a part and to build these into a counterpoint. For instance:

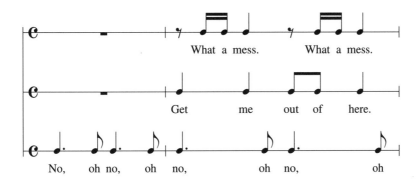

Extension
There is an extension to this activity in the chapter on riffs (see page 82).

LESSON PLAN ♪

Understanding scansion

Poetry has its own rhythm, and a poet writes out the lines in such a way as to make this clear. There is little doubt about the way these famous lines by Wordsworth should be stressed:

    I **wan**dered **lone**ly **as** a **cloud**

This is an example of **iambic** metre: repeated pairs of weak/strong stresses, which a musician might describe as a 'two-in-a-bar'. But – and it is a big 'but' – when we set words to music we do not always follow the implied poetic rhythm, nor do we always keep it regular. The poetic rhythm of the text is called **scansion**, but when music is added there can be many ways of setting the same words. In some cases the scansion suggested by the lyric is changed by the songwriter.

The words of *Stand by Me* (Ben E King) are set to music in a very dramatic way, in short, snatched phrases which are not suggested by the words themselves:

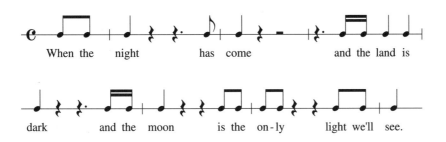

In *Wannabe* (the Spice Girls) the lyrics are very assertive, and this is accentuated by the percussive setting, almost like a military drum:

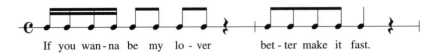

If you wan-na be my lo-ver   bet-ter make it fast.

Listen to *No Woman No Cry* by Bob Marley. Sing the opening phrase and clap the rhythm.

No   wo-man no cry——

Find as many different rhythms as you can to set these words. Examples:

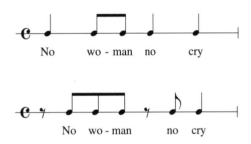

No   wo - man   no   cry

No   wo - man   no   cry

...and one with an anacrusis:

No   wo - man   no   cry

Try the exercise with other phrases from song lyrics.

Pop melody

In *Studying Popular Music* (Open University Press, 1990) the author and academic Richard Middleton has shown that pop melodies fall into types, characterised by the arrangement of the melodic intervals.

Axial

Here the melody moves around a central note:

Examples of axial melodies are:
Nutbush City Limits (Tina Turner)
Like a Prayer (Madonna)
Can't Get You Out of my Head (verse) (Kylie Minogue)
Unchained Melody (various)

Oscillating

The melody alternates between two notes (or two principal notes):

Examples:
Street Fighting Man (Rolling Stones)
Rocking All Over the World (Status Quo)
Wonderwall (Oasis)

The chant

The words are sung to a repeated note (or a series of repeated notes):

Examples:
Night Fever (Bee Gees)
Paradise City (Guns'n Roses)
Put Him Out (Ms Dynamite)

To Middleton's list we can add:

Circular

The melody revolves around a group of three or four notes:

Examples:
  Lucy in the Sky with Diamonds (Beatles)
  The Wall (Pink Floyd)
  When the Going Gets Tough (Billy Ocean)
  Radio Ga Ga (Queen)

Scalic

The melody is based on stepwise motion, drawing its notes from a diatonic scale:

Examples:
  Another Day in Paradise (Phil Collins)
  Karma Chameleon (Culture Club)

Some melodies, whilst not strictly stepwise, are based on a pentatonic (five-note) scale:

Examples:
  You Really Got Me (Kinks)
  Jive Talking (Bee Gees)

Disjunct

The melody is made up predominantly of leaps rather than stepwise movement:

Examples:
  Follow the Sun (Beatles)
  Thank You (Dido)

Chordal

The melody follows a broken chord pattern (for more about chords and how melodies fit with them see Chapter 3):

Examples:
Morning has Broken (Cat Stevens)
D'ya Think I'm Sexy (Rod Stewart)
Walking on the Moon (Police)
I should be so Lucky (chorus) (Kylie Minogue)

LESSON PLAN ♪ and ♫

Listen to the verse and chorus of Madonna's *Like a Prayer*.

Listen to the verse and chorus of the Beatles' *With a Little Help from my Friends*.

Demonstrate on the keyboard that the melodies are based on only five and six notes respectively. The one by the Beatles employs a five-note diatonic scale the outline of which is as follows:

Madonna's is a little more complex:

Working in pairs, choose five or six notes and compose an interesting melody. It may help if it is composed to a simple drum pattern.

Extending melody

In the last section we looked at the types of melodic shapes that form the basis of melody. In this section we will look at common ways of extending melodic ideas into phrases. One of the oldest devices in popular music is **call-and-response** – as used, for instance, in gospel music, where the preacher alternates with choral responses from the congregation. It became an important feature of '60s soul music, two classic examples being Ray Charles' *Hit the Road, Jack* and Solomon Burke's *Everybody Needs Somebody to Love*. A more recent example occurs in the chorus of Bob Marley's *Three Little Birds*, in which Marley, the lead singer, alternates with a prominent keyboard riff.

The idea of call-and-response – a question and answer structure – is rooted in the music of many cultures. An important skill in melody writing is being able to construct an answering phrase to an opening one – a basic **AB** structure and one of the building blocks of musical form.

LESSON PLAN ♪♪

Composing an answering phrase

This lesson is based on a study of two songs, focusing on the structure of the opening melodic phrase.

Listening

Fields of Gold (Sting)
This is in four phrases: three scalic runs answered by a chordal phrase – **AAAB**

With or Without You (U2)
This is in three phrases: two scalic runs answered by a disjunct phrase which includes a downward octave leap – **AAB**

Task

Compose an opening phrase. Choose one of the melody types described above. It may help if you devise the rhythm first. If it is short, you might try repeating it in a similar way to the examples by Sting and U2.

Now add an answering **B** phrase.

Play the whole thing twice through to make a verse.

This lesson links with the chapter on structure – see page 44.

Advanced melody writing

Composers employ a range of devices to make their melodies memorable. These include the **hook**, the **sequence**, and the use of wide intervals to give a melody shape and contour.

The hook

Many songwriters compose their melodies around a hook – so called because it is the feature, usually only a few notes long, which the listener remembers. It is often the musical phrase to which the title words of the song are set. In most cases the composer would choose which words need the hook – normally obvious from the lyrics – and go about writing a catchy motif to go with it.

Three examples of hooks are:

Dry Your Eyes (the Streets)
The hook forms the opening lines of the chorus, to the words 'Dry your eyes, mate', which are sung in contrast to the spoken verses. They are instantly memorable because they employ the first three notes of the scale, giving the melody a simple, nursery-rhyme quality.

Candle in the Wind (Elton John)
The hook is also the title of the song, and is memorable because its setting involves a falling sixth at the end of the phrase on the word 'wind'. This gives the song a rather wistful character.

Wonderwall (Oasis)
This hook is also characterised by a falling interval, a fifth, to the words 'And after *all...*' leading to 'you're my wonderwall'.

Listen, and agree where the hook is. What makes a good hook?

The sequence

The sequence is a common feature in classical music: a phrase is repeated, each repetition being a step higher or lower than the one before. A quick way of illustrating a sequence is to sing the chorus (the 'Gloria' section) of the Christmas carol *Ding Dong Merrily on High*.

Sequences in popular melody tend to be freer than in classical music, although they can be very effective. A striking one occurs in *Life on Mars* (David Bowie), where a phrase (slightly varied each time) gradually ascends over twelve varied repetitions, building to a climax at the chorus.

One song which features a very classical-sounding sequence is the Pet Shop Boys' *Go West*, the reason for this being that it is based on a common classical chord progression – the same one as in Pachelbel's *Canon* (see page 37), a descending phrase pattern over a **cycle of fifths**. There is a similar sequence in Lou Reed's *Perfect Day*, also based on a cycle of fifths. (This song was covered famously by various artists in the 1997 BBC recording for the Children in Need Appeal.) There is an exercise based on the cycle of fifths on page 37.

Other examples:
Fernando (Abba) – ascending sequence
Pinball Wizard (the Who) – descending sequence

The dramatic leap

Some of the best-known songs gain their effect from the overall shape of the melody, in which the range of the singer's voice is exploited to create a sense of drama and climax. The examples below are all singalong anthems, all sharing the same feature: a strong melodic contour, often with a leap at the start of the chorus.

With a Little Help from My Friends (Beatles)
The verse and chorus are built around a simple five-note pattern, but the melody in the middle eight ('Do you need anybody?') leaps up an octave. (Middle eights are discussed in Chapter 4, in the section on 32-bar song form, starting on page 47.) Note that there is also call-and-response between the lead singer and the backing.

Sailing (Rod Stewart)
The opening phrase rises a ninth before falling back to the tonic.

I'm Still Standing (Elton John)
The melody leaps up a seventh at the start of the chorus, and keeps stressing this note.

Angels (Robbie Williams)
The melody in the verse moves largely by step around the tonic. At the chorus it leaps to the highest note in the song.

Yellow (Coldplay)
The melody in the verses is characterised by falling intervals, contrasting with the rising ones in the chorus. Note the wide intervals and disjunct motion of the melody.

The next chapter opens with ideas about linking melody with harmony.

CHAPTER 3

Harmony

In the last chapter we looked at the way melody, rhythm and lyrics are linked together, but there is another element in the relationship: **harmony**.

Melody and harmony

The basic building block of harmony is the triad – a chord of three notes. Triads are easy to work out on the keyboard, because they are played by fingering alternate notes of the scale. On a guitar, the three notes are distributed amongst the six strings, and the guitarist fingers the appropriate 'shape' on the frets.

In the chord shown above, C is called the **root** of the chord. E is the **third** and G is the **fifth**.

Each note has a name: the root, the third (because it is the third note in the scale, counting up from the root) and the fifth (again, named by counting up from the root).

On the next page we will look at the way melody notes can relate to the underlying harmony.

To the teacher

Teachers may wish to explain at this juncture that the notes of the chord can be played in different ways so as to create **inversions**, and they may wish to explain the construction of scales. However, a comprehensive knowledge of scales and the grammar of harmony is not necessary at this stage, although students with a background of formal instrumental tuition will find their knowledge of scales useful. It may prove helpful to refer to a chord dictionary; a good one will show the finger positions for each chord on the keyboard and on the guitar fretboard, the symbol used and the component notes on the stave.

Some of the examples of chord progressions in this chapter have been transposed to keys easier than those on the original records.

In a simple melody the notes may be drawn from those of the underlying chord that forms the backing. In the example below the underlying chord is C major:

The result is an example of a **chordal** melody (see page 25). However, it is more usual to include notes that are not part of the chord. In the next example the stepwise melody includes notes that fit in between, called **passing notes**.

Other ways of decorating the melody include **auxiliary notes**, where a note moves by step from a harmony note and then back again:

Leaps can also be effective, but try to make sure you move onto a harmony note that lies *within* the leap, or the melody may sound awkward.

More complex melodies which feature **dissonance** – notes which deliberately clash with the chord for effect – are discussed later.

The two-chord song

In this lesson, students compose a simple pop song using only two chords.

Equipment	Keyboards, guitars

Listening Songs which are based on two chords, either throughout or for a verse. Examples include:
> *Uptight* Stevie Wonder (D and C)
> *Imagine* John Lennon (C and F)
> *Beat It* Michael Jackson (Dm and C)
> *Everybody Hurts* REM (E and A)

Two-chord patterns are also common in reggae (see Chapter 9).
> *Lively Up Yourself* Bob Marley (D7 and G7)

One artist who has made a feature of the two-chord song is Dido. There are several examples on her album *No Angel*, including:
> *Honestly OK* (Gm7 and Dm7)
> *Slide* (Am7 and Em9)
> *Isobel* (B♭m and E♭m)

Prior learning A small vocabulary of chords based on the examples above and simplified as necessary, for example:
> G and F; C and F; Dm and Am; Em and Dm

Task Working in pairs, devise a two-chord pattern to be played by one student on the lower end of the keyboard. Compose a melody to be played in the treble by the other student.

Hints When devising the chordal backing it may help to invent a rhythm for it first:

Remember that the notes of the chord don't have to be sounded at once:

When adding the melody, think about the notes that make up the chord – it may help to position the hand over these notes.

If the melody starts to wander it may be because the rhythm is dull. Devise a one-bar rhythmic pattern and try playing the notes to that pattern. Another reason may be because the melody lacks structure. It may help to adopt one of the melody types discussed in the previous chapter (see page 23).

Why does pop harmony sound different from classical harmony?

The main reason lies in the historical development of the two styles. The grammar of classical music originates in the sacred vocal counterpoint of the sixteenth century (in which each part was independent), whereas much popular music, especially rock, takes its grammar and idioms from the playing techniques of the guitar (many of which are drawn from Spanish flamenco, and are based on block chords).

Dissonance

In the section above we mentioned how dissonant notes can be added to give colour to the harmony. In some types of classical music these were introduced according to strict rules – for instance the dissonant note was **prepared** (by making it part of a chord with which it is **consonant**); then it sounded as a dissonance on a strong beat; and then **resolved** onto another chord with which it is consonant, on the next beat. Dissonances of this sort are called **suspensions** – here is an example:

In popular music, as in more recent classical music, dissonant notes can be added purely for colour. A chord of C, for example, can be decorated by a dissonant note in several ways:

Dissonance is discussed in more detail later in this chapter.

Inversions

In popular music the bottom note of a chord is usually also the root of the chord. It is possible to place one of the other notes at the bottom – in which case the chord is referred to as an **inversion**. These are not unknown in popular music, but are a much more regular feature of classical music, where they are governed by certain rules.

Chord progressions

Many popular chord progressions include parallel chords, especially in guitar-based songs. These are uncommon in classical music, where they tend to break a fundamental rule by introducing **consecutive fifths** (where two notes of the chord move in parallel, five notes apart). Moreover, the harmony of popular music is often based on modes – especially the *Aeolian* and *Mixolydian*, which both include a flattened leading note.

Lastly, the pentatonic basis of popular music leads to melodies and chord progressions whose sound is unlike that of classical music. Here is a typical example of a rock chord progression built on a pentatonic root-note sequence:

A   C   D   F   G

LISTENING ♩♪

Chord progressions in popular music often occur as a repeating cycle of 2, 4 or 8 bars (see below). These structures are rare in classical music, where the flow is punctuated by regular cadences.

The difference between classical and popular harmony can be heard clearly in Abba's *Lay All Your Love on Me*, which combines a dance groove with a Bach pastiche. The change of style from the chorus to the verse is very striking.

The verses are harmonised by a simple two-chord pattern (Dm and C) over a dance groove, whilst the chorus is in the style of a Bach chorale: two four-bar phrases with an imperfect cadence at the end of the first phrase and a perfect cadence (modulating to the relative major) at the end of the second. The setting of the words in the chorus is entirely syllabic, with one chord per syllable. For students of classical harmony it is worth noting that this is only a pastiche and breaks several rules: the published song sheet version includes a consecutive fifth, and all the chords but one are in root position.

Chord progressions

Two-bar patterns

We have already studied the two-chord song. To this we can add the three-chord riff. This is a guitar-based pattern consisting of three chords spread over two bars and repeated continually as the backing of a song.

What can make the riff interesting is the **harmonic rhythm**, for example when the first bar has only one chord and the next has two. Many guitarists will control the strum pattern to vary the rhythmic articulation of the chords.

Examples of three-chord riffs:

| G F | C | *Midnight Rambler* (Rolling Stones)

| Am | F G | *Dirty Diana* (Michael Jackson)

| C F | G | *Twist and Shout* (Isley Bros, Beatles)

The three-chord riff was a particular favourite of Lou Reed. Two of his songs based on this pattern are *Sweet Jane* and *Walk on the Wild Side*. Examples by other composers include:

Purple Haze (Jimi Hendrix)
Baba O'Riley (The Who)
Summer Loving (from the musical *Grease*)
Anarchy in the UK (Sex Pistols)
Park Life (Blur)

In some songs the riff lasts more than two bars but still uses three chords, the repeated chord featuring a driving guitar riff with a two-chord change later in the phrase. Examples:

Money for Nothing (Dire Straits)
| Em | Em | Em | C D |

Steamy Windows (Tina Turner)
| Em | Em | G D | Em |

Four-bar patterns

This is one of the commonest structures in popular music: four bars with one chord per bar. Many four-bar patterns have become stock progressions, used over and over again by songwriters.

C Am F G   *I Will Always Love You* (Whitney Houston)
              Unchained Melody (various artists)

C Am Dm G   *Closest Thing to Crazy* (Katie Melua)

C Em F G   *Crocodile Rock* (Elton John)
              Live and Let Die (Paul McCartney)

C G Am F   *Let it Be* (Beatles)
              No Woman No Cry (Bob Marley)
              With or Without You (U2)

C F Dm7 G and C D F G   *Strong* (Robbie Williams)

D F C D   *Sympathy for the Devil* (Rolling Stones, Guns'n Roses)

Em Am G C   *Smells Like Teenage Spirit* (Nirvana)

C D Bm7 Em *Boring* (Pet Shop Boys)

Am G F E   *Good Vibrations* (Beach Boys)

Eight-bar patterns

Many eight-bar progressions form part of a larger ballad (for example, in the ballads of Carole King, Elton John and Billy Joel, and in many examples of 32-bar song form – see page 47). However, there are examples of songs which are based on a repeated eight-bar pattern. In some cases these are the result of chaining two- and four-bar patterns together, but some last the full eight bars.

House of the Rising Sun (trad., version by the Animals)
Am C D F Am C E E

Hotel California (Eagles)
Am E G D F C Dm E

Stairway to Heaven (Led Zeppelin)
Am E/G♯ G D/F♯ F G Am Am

Roxanne (the Police)
Gm Dm/F E♭maj7 Dm Cm Fsus4 Gsus4 Gsus4
This pattern looks more complex than it really is. For the first five chords the bass simply descends stepwise: G F E♭ D C

Don't Look Back in Anger (Oasis)
C G Am E F G C G

Go West (Pet Shop Boys), *Streets of London* (Ralph McTell)
C G Am Em F C Dm G

Perfect Day (Lou Reed)
Am D G C F Bdim E E

Hey Joe (Jimi Hendrix)
C G D A E E E

The last two examples are built on a pattern called the **cycle of fifths**. The bass line follows a sequence in which the root falls or rises by five notes each time.

To the teacher

Study Project 1, starting on the next page, is about designing chord charts to show the sorts of progressions described above. Simple chord charts for the classroom can be constructed using the 'draw table' function in Microsoft Word, or by some similar method. These can be printed off and used as worksheets for students to complete patterns, design their own, and chain them together to make a song (see also Chapter 12).

1 Designing a chord chart

Studio musicians rarely work from a full score but instead use a chart, a list of chords which is written out so as to show the structure of the song. The player is expected to provide the correct feel and fill in the part with improvised passages as required.

Look at the charts below, and find chords to complete the patterns. Each box represents one bar.

Two-chord patterns

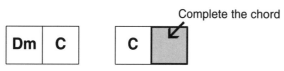

Four-chord patterns

Eight-chord patterns

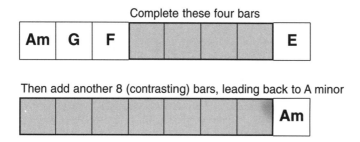

Chord patterns like these can be connected together to make the sections of a song:

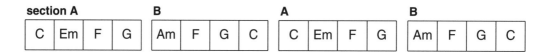

An eight-bar pattern can be created by chaining together two four-bar ones and then varying the last two chords:

Don't forget that the harmonic rhythm can be changed. This adds interest and movement to the song (remind yourself by playing through the three-chord riffs above – see page 33).

2 Pachelbel's Canon

The famous chord progression from Pachelbel's *Canon* (and used by the Pet Shop Boys and Ralph McTell – see above, page 35) forms the basis of the following exercise in building a melody around a chord progression.

First, learn the chords:

C G Am Em F C Dm G

If you are working with a partner, you can take it in turns to play the chords while the other devises a melody. If you are working alone you may find it easier to play just the root note as a bass line:

Next, add a melody based on the notes of the chord. You may find that the melody will fall into a sequence.

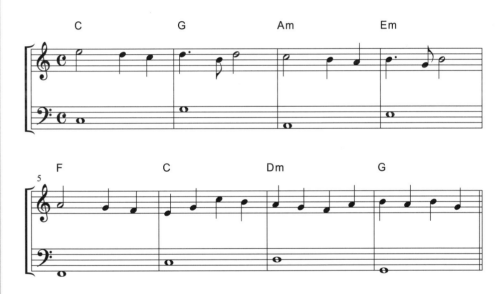

Try the same process with other chord progressions. You will find that chords based on harmonic sequences like this will almost always support a sequential melody.

3 New melody, old chords

Choose any well-known pop song and write out the chord progression in the form of a simple chord chart. Play through the chords (it may be easier just to play the root notes). Either working in pairs or alone, have a go at composing a *new* melody to fit the chords.

4 Countermelodies

The art of combining melodies is known as **counterpoint**. It is much used in classical music, but is also a feature of many pop songs, usually where a counter-melody is added to the main melody, or where the backing vocals each have a different part. One way of learning to write counterpoint is to try exercises based on **species counterpoint**.

Start with a simple bass line:

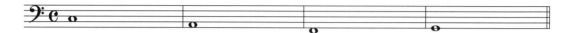

Then add a melody line, note against note:

Now add a second melody in minims:

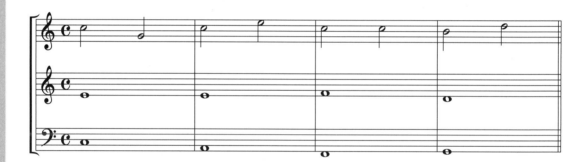

And a third one in crotchets:

Try swapping the parts round so the crotchets are in an inner part and the semi-breves are at the top.

Following the above procedure, choose a simple chord progression and try adding two melodies to it, one in long notes and the other in shorter ones with more rhythmic movement.

5 Writing a bass line

The composer Henry Mancini once said that the bass line is as important as the melody. Composing a good bass line requires an understanding of harmony.

The opening section of this chapter showed how a melody may include non-essential notes – notes that do not belong to the chord, such as passing notes and auxiliaries. A bass line is constructed using the same principles. The root of the chord is usually placed on (or near) the first beat, and the bass player adds rhythmic and melodic interest in the rest of the bar.

The following exercise is related to the counterpoint exercises above.

Choose a chord progression and write (or play) a bass line consisting of the roots of the chords:

Now add notes to join the long notes together as a melodic line:

...or you could introduce a rhythmic pattern:

You can also try composing a **walking bass**, all in crotchets:

Dissonance

Dissonance can give added interest to harmony. The dissonance can arise in the melody (so it clashes with the bass) or dissonant notes can be included in the chords themselves.

In addition to adding notes to chords as shown on page 32, the basic triad can be extended by continuing to add 3rds.

For instance, in the major:

...and in the minor:

To get the effect of some of these chords, it may not be necessary to play all the notes, as the following examples show:

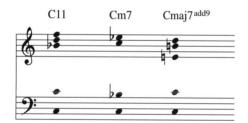

Chords with a lot of dissonant notes are more characteristic of jazz than pop music, but they can provide colour. This is especially in pop styles which draw some of their influences from jazz, like R&B and garage, where the chords often consist of parallel sevenths:

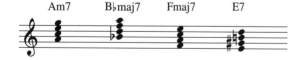

To the teacher

Some students may find it helpful at this stage to be guided through the structure of scales and intervals. Others may feel more comfortable experimenting with a chord dictionary.

It is also possible to decorate an otherwise simple chord progression:

| C | F | Dm | G | |

...can become:

| C | Fmaj7 | Dm7 | G11 | |

...or:

| C | Fmaj7 | A♭maj7 | G♭9 | |

In the last version, the A♭ chord is known as a **substitution chord** because it replaces the original D minor one. This is an example of a **tritone substitution**, so called because the root of the new chord (A♭) is a tritone (i.e. a diminished 5th) away from the original (D). Substitution chords are best found by experimenting. There are a few simple guidelines: exchange minor for major (and vice versa); change to chords with notes in common (e.g. E minor for C); try changing the root by a tritone. Tritone substitutions are often employed where there is a cycle of fifths:

| C G | Em Am | Dm G | C |

With substitutions:

| C G | Em E♭ | Dm G | C |

Dissonance in the melody

A melody which contains notes that clash with the bass can have great emotional power. Two examples of songs where this occurs are *My Heart Will Go On* (sung by Celine Dion, from the film *Titanic*) and *Will You Still Love Me Tomorrow?* (Carole King).

Just as we can decorate a chord by adding a dissonance, so we can decorate a melody:

Note that the dissonant note almost always **resolves** onto the note above or, more usually, below, thus following some of the rules of classical harmony. If it doesn't resolve like this, the melody may sound very angular:

There are some instances, however, where most of the melody notes are dissonant. The one below is in a typical R&B style:

The harmony is D minor and B♭, but the melody follows the notes of A minor. This is an example of what jazz musicians call **playing away from the chord**, and is common in modern jazz. An example of a melody like this occurs in *Venus as a Boy* by Björk.

It is possible to play away from the chord by changing the harmony over a **pedal** (an unchanging note, usually in the bass) lasting a whole phrase, an effect of which Phil Collins and the Pet Shop Boys are fond:

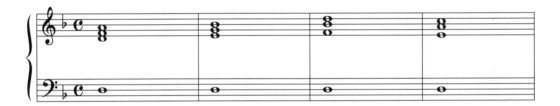

or by repeating a melodic idea and changing the chords beneath (a favourite device of U2):

EXERCISE ♪♪♪

Start with any standard four-bar chord progression and compose a melody which includes dissonant notes. Think which notes will be dissonant – most instances of dissonance follow 'classical' rules, the fourth, seventh and ninth notes above the bass note being the most common, and sounding on a strong beat.

You may find it easier to play just the root note of the chord on a keyboard and to stick to the **primary triads** (chords I, IV and V). Remind yourself what key you are in, and what the notes of the scale are.

More skilled performers might try an accompaniment pattern such as broken chords or a strummed pattern on the guitar.

Extension (for the adventurous)
Try an eight-bar pattern like the one based on Pachelbel's *Canon*.

LESSON PLAN ♪♪♪

Harmonising a melody

Most of the exercises in this chapter have focused on the chords as a starting point for a melody. In this lesson the student approaches the problem the other way round – by starting with the melody.

Using a simple one-bar percussion pattern as a guide, compose an eight-bar melody. Keyboard players may find it easier to use only white notes. Guitarists working with a singer in an unfamiliar key may find a capo helpful.

Now add chords to the melody. There are two main approaches you can adopt:

➤ Work out the likely chords from the melody notes.

➤ Trial and error, starting with the primary triads and then replacing these with more varied chords. (This is not as hit and miss as it may seem at first, since the first chord is almost certain to be the tonic.)

The next chapter opens with ideas about linking harmony with structure.

CHAPTER 4

Structure

Harmony and structure

There is more to harmony than providing a framework of chords as a basis for the melody. It is also employed by songwriters to articulate the structure of the song. An example of this is when composers raise the key by a semitone in the final verse or chorus. This provides lift and climax, giving the singer an opportunity to hit higher notes.

Examples of this device occur in many big love ballads:
   I Got You Babe (Sonny and Cher)
   I Will Always Love You (Whitney Houston)
   My Heart Will Go On (Celine Dion)

The importance of the dominant chord

All keys have a **dominant** chord – the triad that is built on the fifth note of the scale. The dominant is important because it often has the function of leading back to the **tonic** chord (the one from which the key takes its name, and which is built on the first note of the scale). For example, in the key of C, C is the tonic and G is the dominant.

A chord progression which finishes dominant–tonic has a feeling of finality, and this is called a **perfect cadence**:

   C   Am   Dm   G   C

One which finishes on a dominant chord without a tonic resolution has no sense of finality, and is called an **imperfect cadence**:

   C   F   C   G

Three-chord riffs (see page 33) in which the last chord is the dominant always have a feeling of forward motion:

   |C   F |G |

This special property of the dominant chord is exploited by songwriters to help create structure, for example to set up a chorus.

PROJECT ♪♪♪

Devising a simple song backing with a chorus

This may involve several lessons with homework to polish up a final performance.

Equipment
Keyboards, guitars, or a computer sequencing package.

Prior learning
Remind yourself about building chord progressions, as this project builds on the

exercises in the previous chapter, particularly those involving the construction of a chord chart.

Task

Compose a set of chords to make up a verse/chorus structure based on the example below. This is a standard pattern: a 16-bar verse followed by a 16-bar chorus.

The **verse** should have two four-bar phrases answered by a second pair of four-bar phrases – an **AABB** pattern, 16 bars in all.

In the example below, the **A** phrase includes a variation in the harmonic rhythm, and the **B** phrase shifts to a contrast of harmony and ends on the dominant chord. Such a passage, which links the verse to the chorus, is sometimes called a **pre-chorus** or **bridge.**

Verse

A				A				B				B			
C	F	G	C	C	F	G	C	Am	G	F	G	Am	G	F	G

The **chorus** has four four-bar phrases, making 16 bars in all. In the example, there is a passing modulation through A minor in the middle of the chorus; you may wish to do something similar. All students should aim to have a perfect cadence at the end.

Chorus

C				D				E				F			
C	Em	F	G	C	F	Bdim	E	Am	F	Dm	G	C	G	C	C

Hints

Aim at a simple backing at first, bringing life to the chords by using interesting keyboard figurations or strumming patterns on the guitar.

If you take up the challenge of including a passing modulation, the key to be passed through will need to be set up by *its* dominant. In the example the key is A minor, so this needs to be preceded by an E major chord. This chord is, in turn, preceded by B diminished. This is known as a **pivot chord**, because it belongs both to C major and A minor. B is also five notes higher up the scale than E, so it acts as a 'dominant' preparation for the E major chord. Students of classical harmony will recognise this as a II–V–I cadence with the bass rising in fourths – always a strong progression.

The chords in the example are all basic triads, but don't forget that these can be decorated by adding sevenths, ninths, etc. The dominant chords in bar 16 leading to the chorus, and at the final cadence in bar 30 of the chorus, would benefit from an added seventh. You could also try adding sevenths to some of the minor chords.

Development 1   Try adding a melody.

Development 2   Study some of the songs analysed in Chapter 7, in particular:
    Gershwin: *A Foggy Day*
    Beatles: *Penny Lane, Come Together*
    Elton John: *Philadelphia Freedom, Can You Feel the Love Tonight?*

Standard structures

Strophic

A strophic form is one in which the words are different in each verse but the melody is repeated. It is quite rare in popular music just to have verses and no chorus, but it is more common in folk music. Most of the examples of strophic form that have made it into the charts are traditional or by folk-influenced artists:

House of the Rising Sun (The Animals)
Mr Tambourine Man (Bob Dylan, also covered by the Byrds)
Sound of Silence and *Scarborough Fair* (Simon and Garfunkel)

One rock songwriter who has had successful hits with strophic songs is Rod Stewart, two notable examples being *Maggie May* (which has a seamless 24-bar melody) and *Sailing*.

The twelve-bar blues

This is a traditional pattern, determined by the progression of the three **primary triads** – that is, the three major triads which are found on the first, fourth and fifth degrees of the scale. For this reason the blues is an ideal starting point to learn the basics of harmony. In C major the structure is as follows:

| |C | | | |F | |C | |G | |C | | |

The last four bars can take different forms, sometimes being known as the **turn-around** when the dominant chord prepares the way for the next verse.

|G |F |C |C	
|G |F |C |G	
|G |F |Dm |G	
|G |G |C Am|F G	

The twelve-bar blues formed the basis of early blues, rhythm and blues and rock'n'roll, and can be heard in the songs of Chuck Berry (e.g. *Johnny B Goode*) and John Lee Hooker (e.g. *Boom Boom*), as well as the first ever rock'n'roll number 1 hit, Bill Haley's *Rock around the Clock*. Although the twelve-bar blues is not heard as commonly in the charts today, it has featured in several successful hits, including:

Can't Buy Me Love (Beatles)
Let's Work Together (Wilbert Harrison, covered by Bryan Ferry)
U Got the Look (Prince)
Billie Jean (Michael Jackson)
Never Ever (All Saints)

A great deal of popular music is blues-based, even if it doesn't follow the twelve-bar pattern exactly. This listening activity will help you to recognise the primary triads.

Preparatory task
Perform a twelve-bar blues.

Main task
Identify the order of chords I, IV and V in the following songs. All are blues-based but follow 8- and 16-bar patterns. Draw a chart and write in the Roman numerals. For instance, your chart could look like this:

I		IV		I	V	I	V

The advantage of using Roman numerals is that these apply irrespective of the key of the song.

Try these two eight-bar blues patterns:
Rockin' all over the world (Status Quo)
Heartbreak Hotel (Elvis Presley)

Now a harder one, 16 bars long:
Fun, Fun, Fun (Beach Boys)

Answers on page 78

32-bar song form

This is the form of many jazz standards and show songs of the '30s and '40s. It is based on classical **ternary form**, being an **AABA** structure, and is thought to have developed alongside the technology of the early wind-up gramophone where it was possible to get two 32-bar verses onto one side of a 12-inch record.

In its classic form its four phrases are each eight bars long – hence the 32-bar name. Crucial to the form is the **B** section – the **middle eight** – which typically opens with a contrast of harmony (or even a key change) and normally finishes on the home dominant chord to prepare for the return to the **A** section.

The basic structure is illustrated below:

A
:							:

B
							chord V

A

The **A** section sometimes has 1st and 2nd time bars, with varied chords to set up a change of key in the B section:

A

| | | | | | | | |1 |2 |
|:|:|:|:|:|:|:|:|:|:|

B

A

32-bar form is not so common today, but it does feature in some very successful songs, including *Every Breath You Take* (the Police) and *Yesterday* (the Beatles). Many of the early Beatles songs were cast in **AABA** form – though not necessarily with eight bars in each section. Here are some examples – Beatles songs and some others:

Yesterday
When I'm Sixty Four
Penny Lane
Here There and Everywhere
Eight Days a Week
A Hard Day's Night
From Me to You

Everyday, Raining in My Heart (Buddy Holly)
I Only Want to Be With You (Dusty Springfield)
Close to You (the Carpenters – see also page 91)
You are the Sunshine of My Life (Stevie Wonder)
Many Rivers to Cross (Jimmy Cliff)
All Right (Supergrass)

Many early pop songs simply repeat the **AABA** structure throughout, usually including an instrumental verse or two (it was customary for the singer to come back in for the middle eight). More recent songs have been more elaborate: *Every Breath You Take* and *All Right* both include a second middle section.

In *Every Breath You Take* the new middle section (which is ten bars long) enters after the first **AABA** and before the second. The second **AABA** starts as an instrumental, with the vocals re-entering at the B section:

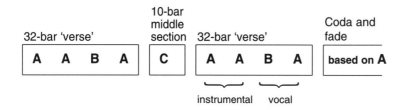

The **coda** is a short 'tailpiece' to finish off the song. Some songs, like this one, have a coda *and* a fade-out at the end.

The key to writing a good 32-bar song is a strong middle eight. This needs to open with contrasting harmony (as well as a contrasting melody) and have a convincing return by setting up the dominant chord carefully – in fact these are the rules for *most* middle sections, which is why 32-bar form is a good one to study.

Choice of harmony for the middle eight can be quite simple – e.g. a change of key to the subdominant (the fourth degree of the scale) or the relative minor (sixth degree). Some songs feature quite remote changes. The tables below, in the keys of C and C minor respectively, show some of the possible keys for the middle eight, and the chords likely to be used to modulate to them in the second time bar. It is worth remembering that not all composers bother to modulate, preferring to jump into the new key unexpectedly. Either is possible, but always try out your chords to check whether or not they make sense.

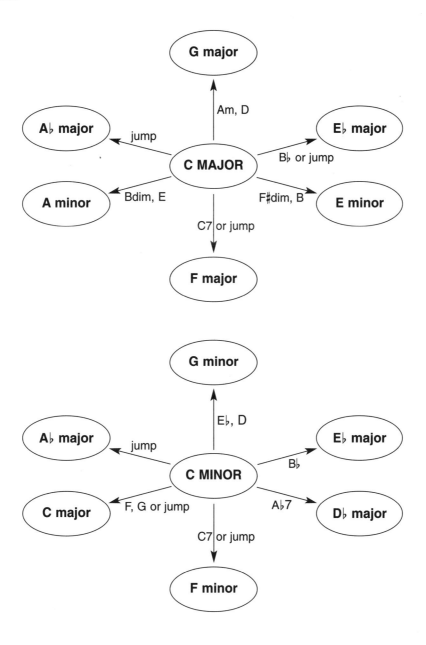

Note the tonic major (at the eight o'clock position in the lower diagram). It is easier than you think to jump between major and minor modes: the classical symphonists did it all the time.

Getting back again

Returning to the home key is the hard part because you only have eight bars in which to do it. Sometimes it helps to work backwards. You know you need to end up on the dominant chord of the original key, so you could try one of these formulae:

➤ Divide the eight bars into two and try some standard four-bar progressions.

➤ A cycle of fifths is a strong progression – try one and see where you end up. (Or work backwards in fifths from the chord on which you want to end.)

➤ Try parallel chords – a descending progression can be made to lead almost anywhere, e.g. F, Em, E♭, Dm, G

EXERCISES ♪♪ to ♪♪♪♪

Practice at writing a middle eight is a useful aid to songwriting. It also helps in learning how harmony works. Here are some ideas for exercises, starting with simpler ones.

♪♪

Using a chord chart, compile a simple verse using four-bar progressions. Use a contrasting progression for the middle eight, but try to ensure that the last chord is a dominant one so it sets up the repeat.

Example:

							Fine							*D.C. al Fine*
‖: C	Am	F	G ‖	C	F	G	C :‖	F	G	C	Am	F	Dm	G	G ‖

Students who have worked the example on page 45 should note that the dominant was employed there to set up a chorus. The 32-bar song is different, both because it involves a middle eight and because the dominant is employed to set up the return to the **A** section.

♪♪♪

➤ Working in pairs, each student chooses a song with a middle eight from a song book. Copy out the middle eight, in chord chart form, leaving out a few bars from the end or the middle. Swap your charts and try to complete the chords. Try to guess what the original composer did – or put in chords of your own.

➤ Play through only the A section of a song and try to write a *new* middle eight.

♪♪♪♪

➤ Write out the chords of the A section, and see how many different second time bars you can compose, each going to a different key.

➤ Plan a 'route map' from one key to another – for example you could start in a remote key and try to find your way back in eight bars.

Some final thoughts about middle eights

A successful middle eight does not *have* to involve a change of harmony or key. Variety can be achieved in other ways:

➤ Change the harmonic rhythm – if the harmonies of the verses consist of one chord per bar, try doubling it (two per bar) or halving it (one every two bars), or use a mixture of the two.

➤ Change the backing rhythm, for example the drum pattern.

➤ Change the instrumentation.

➤ Change the melody – if the melody of the verse is based predominantly on scalic figurations then try chordal ones.

Verse and chorus

This is the most common strong structure of all. Typically, the chorus follows after one or two verses. It is often set up by a short **pre-chorus** or **bridge** which occupies the second half of the verse and, like a middle eight, closes on a dominant chord to build expectation for the chorus.

Some songwriters refer to a middle eight as a bridge – it is a flexible term. The soul singer James Brown would often call to the band 'Take me to the bridge', but what the band actually played was a standard middle eight.

Analysis

Strong (Robbie Williams) is a verse-and-chorus song with several twists to prevent it from being predictable as a structure.

The basic structure consists of:
    Intro
    Verse 1, Bridge, Chorus
    Verse 2, Bridge, Chorus
    Middle
    Instrumental (based on chorus)
    Bridge (vocals re-enter)
    Chorus (four times, as described below)

Introduction
Based on the chorus.

Verse 1
Two four-bar phrases. Each ends on a dominant chord, which pushes the song along. At the end of the second phrase the lyrics point clearly to the next section ('That's a good line to take it to the bridge').

Bridge
Four bars. Jumps into relative minor and ends on the home dominant as a preparation for the chorus. Melody more animated.

Chorus
Two four-bar phrases. Note how the melody has climbed so as to climax at its highest point at the start of the chorus.

Repeat Verse, Bridge, Chorus

Middle
Ten bars (8+2).

Instrumental
Based on the chorus.

Bridge
A vocal re-entry in the bridge after an instrumental is standard song practice. Here, the bridge is extended from the original four bars to five.

Chorus
Three times, then fades: the first time straight, the second time with backing vocals and the third time overlaid with elements of the verse.

ACTIVITIES ♪♪♪

1 Devise three eight-bar chord patterns by chaining together two four-bar ones: one for a verse, one for a chorus and one for a middle. Now compose melodies over these chords. Try to make the verse simple, the chorus memorable and the middle contrasting.

2 Choose a favourite song and devise either an introduction or a coda.

LISTENING ♪♪ and ♪♪♪

Some songs seem to break all the rules with regard to structure, and that makes them all the more interesting. This is a listening exercise based on the commentary type of question commonly found in music exams.

Students are encouraged to use technical terminology and to focus on the way in which specific elements of the music – for example rhythm, melody, harmony, instrumentation and style – are employed to create structure.

The three songs can be played one after the other (and compared), or the teacher can choose one for special discussion.

Bohemian Rhapsody (Queen)

This has been cited as one of the great rock anthems, and is one of the longest running chart hits. Apart from being one of the longest singles ever released, it broke new ground as a pop song:

➤ It is in every sense a rhapsody – a free form with little repetition whose broad structure is **A B C A**.

➤ There is neither a chorus nor a middle, although the original melody returns at the very end to form a short coda.

➤ Rapid changes of musical style through ballad, opera pastiche (with *a cappella* vocals) and heavy guitar climax (very popular as an 'air guitar' solo) – note the shuffle rhythm.

Love and Affection (Joan Armatrading)

Joan Armatrading is a songwriter with a folk-blues style that draws on a wide range of influences. This song builds from a simple start:

➤ An introductory phrase builds into a verse with a clear backing pattern strummed on the guitar and repeated to establish a second verse.

➤ These opening verses prove only to be an introduction (they are never repeated), and lead to the establishment of a three-chord guitar riff, taken up by the other instruments, which grows in strength to dominate the rest of the song.

➤ There is a clearly defined and contrasting middle section, although the vocal part remains free and improvisatory.

➤ The saxophone solo signals the end of the song, followed by a final return of the vocals over the three-chord riff.

Rockafella Skank (Fatboy Slim, aka Norman Cook)

This is a song built from samples (see pages 119–122). Cook does not compose songs, so much as assemble them from sampled material. *Rockafella Skank* is based on a looped vocal sample (a rap) and this is repeated throughout the song. It is really a free **rondo**, with episodes which either treat the original sample electronically or add new backing patterns.

The basic structure is as follows:
    Rap, building to drums and guitar
    Rap, with 2-chord guitar pattern
    Guitar solo
    Rap
    New guitar riff
    Rap, slowing down
    A tempo, with new drum pattern, then rap speeding up
    Repeat guitar riff
    Rap sample breaks down

Task

Write a short commentary on the structure of one of the three songs above. Alternatively, choose another song with an unconventional structure, and analyse it in a similar way.

Highlighting the chorus

Songwriters adopt a range of devices to make the chorus memorable. Here are some examples.

Starting with the chorus

Whilst the majority of songs open with the verse (perhaps after an introduction), some songwriters have exploited the drama of opening with the chorus which, because it usually contains the strongest material, gets the song off to a bold start.

Examples
> *Dancing Queen* and *Super Trouper* (Abba)
> *Three Little Birds* (Bob Marley)
> *You Can Get It if you Really Want* (Jimmy Cliff)

The contrasting chorus

A chorus which moves into a new tempo or adopts a contrasting stylistic feel can be very effective.

Changes (David Bowie)
Has a verse with a strong jazz/ballad feel and a rock chorus.

Stan (Eminem)
This song broke new ground in taking the chorus of another song, sampled and woven into the production. The chorus was from Dido's *Thank you*, and the adaptation helped launch her career. In contrast with these sung passages the verses are rapped by Eminem.

Of all songwriters, Sting has perhaps experimented the most with different styles. Several hits by the Police follow this pattern:
> *Every Little Thing She Does is Magic* – ballad verse and calypso chorus
> *Roxanne* – reggae verse and rock chorus
> *So Lonely* – ballad verse and rock chorus

The understated chorus

Last but not least, it is worth remembering that choruses do not have to be prominent. Some are effective because they are woven into the song, flowing logically from the verses without standing out like a fanfare:

Examples
> *Heaven Knows I'm Miserable Now* (Smiths)
> *Scar Tissue* (Red Hot Chilli Peppers)
> *Fake Plastic Trees* (Radiohead)
> *Trouble* (Coldplay)

> The next chapter opens with ideas about linking structure with instrumentation.

CHAPTER 5

Instruments

A study of instrumentation is important for two reasons. First, a knowledge of instruments and their capabilities helps in the creation of an interesting arrangement. The structure of a song can be enhanced by changes in texture and chordal figuration – a chorus, for example, can be given extra presence with the addition of a string section, or by changing the guitar part from finger style to power chords. Instruments and their combinations are discussed below.

Another important reason for studying instrumentation is that many of the listening tests in exams require an ability to identify instruments and instrumental effects. A popular type of question involves comparing two performances of the same song, and the differences between the two are often instrumental. This is covered in more detail in Part III.

It is not possible to cover the subject in detail here, so a good orchestration manual is recommended. One of the best ones for popular music and jazz is Henry Mancini's *Sounds and Scores* (Music Sales, 1997).

LISTENING ♪

In both the following songs, the imaginative use of instruments is the main feature of the production. For example, both avoid the use of a conventional drum kit, and both are structured around contrasts of timbre and the build up of textures.

God Only Knows (Beach Boys)
Recorded in 1966 and included in the ground-breaking *Pet Sounds* album. Brian Wilson was a great experimenter and his originality shows in *God Only Knows* with its unusual instrumentation and vocal counterpoint.

Isobel (Björk)
Björk is also an innovator. This song from 1995 includes an unusual drum backing and a lush string arrangement. Melodically and harmonically it is quite simple, but the changes of timbre and texture sustain the listener's interest.

List the instruments you can hear in each of these songs.

Answers on page 78

The instruments of popular music

The guitar

The six-string guitar is, for many, the mainstay of popular music. The guitar was the chosen instrument of many of the early blues singers, and many of the 'heroes' of rock are guitar virtuosi: Jimi Hendrix, Eric Clapton, Jimmy Page, Eddie Van Halen, Slash, Brian May.

The strings are tuned (from the lowest upwards) to E, A, D, G, B, E – although other tunings are possible. The acoustic version (sometimes called the Spanish guitar) can be strung with nylon or metal strings, and there is a twelve-string version which has a very rich sound. Some acoustic guitars include a **pickup** – a magnetic device lying beneath the strings – so the instrument can be connected to an amplifier.

There are a number of ways of playing the guitar: **strumming** (with or without a plectrum) and **finger style**, when individual strings are picked out. Some blues styles employ a **bottleneck**, nowadays a metal tube rather than a real bottleneck, which, when placed over the finger and pressed against the fretboard, allows *glissando* effects.

The electric guitar will only work when connected to an amplifier, and its sound is often enhanced by the use of **outboards** – effects operated by a foot pedal. The most common are:

Distortion	creates a powerful, harsh effect, common in heavy rock
Compression	sustains the sound, good for solo work
Chorus	thickens the sound, atmospheric for ballads

LISTENING ♪♪♪

Examples of instrumental work are best studied by listening. One band whose work is driven by inventive guitar work is U2.

Pride (in the Name of Love)
The chorus is accompanied by a fast semiquaver strum on the top strings only. Notice how the cymbal part in the drums is kept simple so as not to clutter up the rhythm, leaving the guitar free to drive the song forwards. In the verses the texture changes to arpeggiated chords with a chorus effect.

Numb
Here the guitar is played through a **gate**, an electronic switch which opens to allow the sound through at a predetermined level. This has the effect of cutting off the beginning and ending of the player's strum so the sound begins abruptly and percussively, more like a piano. The guitar is also heavily distorted. Note how, as the gate closes on some of the chords, the partials change to create a **sweep** effect.

The bass guitar and double bass

For many composers and producers the bass is the most important part – Henry Mancini, in his *Sounds and Scores*, has said that the bass line should be composed with as much care and attention as the melody.

Most bass guitars have four strings, tuned to E, A, D, G. Some have a fifth string, a B below the bottom E. The **fretless bass** is popular amongst jazz players, and has a slightly less percussive sound, but it is also possible to soften the sound of a fretted bass by fitting **flat-wound** strings; the string is wound with flat wire rather than the usual rounded wire so it has a softer profile (and is also gentler on the fingers). The (acoustic) **double bass** is popular with rock'n'roll and country and western bands, and was featured memorably on Lou Reed's *Walk on the Wild Side*.

Usually the bass guitar is played by being plucked, although some styles of funk feature **thumbs** (where the player taps the string percussively with the side of the thumb) and **slaps** (where the finger is hooked under the string and released to create a snap pizzicato). Generally these techniques together are known as **slap bass** style, and can be heard on recordings by Weather Report, Level 42 and Jamiroquai.

Going unplugged

In recent years there has been a trend towards acoustic performances, and away from the excesses of stadium rock and its towering banks of loudspeakers. One memorable instance of a band going unplugged was when Bon Jovi appeared as buskers with an acoustic set in London's Covent Garden market.

There are many virtues in keeping it simple. A song can benefit from understatement. *That's Entertainment* is one of Paul Weller's best known songs, but he chose to record it with acoustic instruments rather than the Jam's usual amplified line-up: the anger and irony of the lyrics comes across all the more strongly.

Drums

The basic kit of snare drum, hi-hat cymbals and bass drum creates the three-part drum texture discussed in Chapter 1. To these are usually added **top toms**, tom-toms arranged around the top of the bass drum, and **floor toms**. Some players have a set of eight, tuned to the diatonic scale, and in heavy rock bands these are occasionally fitted with oil-filled skins to give a heavier, deader sound. Drummers often experiment with muffles and mutes to get the sound they want. A wide range of sticks is also available.

In addition to the hi-hat there is usually a **crash cymbal** and a **ride cymbal**. The ride cymbal is thicker and heavier, and acts as an alternative for beating out a quaver pulse (especially the 'swing' rhythm – see page 12). Some kits also include a **splash cymbal** (for small crashes, rather circus-like), a **china cymbal** (with a deeper tone) and a **rivet cymbal** (with rivets fitted loosely round the rim, helping to thicken and sustain the sound – sometimes called **sizzle cymbal**).

The development of electronic percussion has added to the drummer's range of instruments. Many kits include **drum pads** – flat panels with the bounce and feel of an acoustic drum, but where the stick triggers a MIDI signal (see page 67) to produce electronic drum sounds. A set of digital drums will be entirely electronic, with a set of pads attached to a frame and a module of sounds to tune the drums and select different types of kit (e.g. heavy, jazz, electronic).

Piano and keyboards

The piano has been the instrument of choice for many singer-songwriters including Carole King, Billy Joel, Elton John and Alicia Keys, all of whom sing while playing the instrument. The keyboard has also been the principal means of inputting musical data into a computer; some bands, notably the Pet Shop Boys, consist *only* of a singer and keyboardist who records all the backing parts, only bringing in special instrumentalists when needed. The use of the computer in this way will be discussed below.

The piano is actually a very difficult instrument to record well – some studio engineers cite the piano introduction to Dusty Springfield's *I Close My Eyes and Count to Ten* (1968) as an example of recording excellence. Nowadays producers are more likely to employ a digital piano – the sounds produced, using samples from high-quality pianos (e.g. Steinways or Bechsteins), are so sophisticated that the average listener would find it hard to tell the difference, and an electronic piano has the advantage of plugging directly into the recording system without the need to be miked up. The same applies to the organ, an instrument that today is likely be replaced by a synthesiser – although an original Hammond organ (with its Lesley rotary speaker system) is considered something of a collector's item, and its retro sound is sought after.

The modern synthesiser with its sampled sounds can imitate most instruments, but, as with most commodities, you get what you pay for. Usually synthesisers are employed either to provide a solo using a strident timbre (such as a synth lead or brass) or to fill in the background with chordal support using string sounds or a **pad** (a synthesised and sustained timbre). To make synth parts more interesting it is worth considering the following points:

➤ Can the timbre be doubled with another to create a blend? The more expensive synthesisers can be programmed, and it is always worth experimenting. Can you soften the start of the note by slowing down the **attack**? Can you make it last longer by extending the **release**? Both of these functions are usually adjustable using the **envelope shaper**.

➤ Can you make the part more interesting rhythmically? A series of sustained chords, all of them on the beat, can be very tiring for the listener.

Arranging chords

Chords are given added interest by the way they are articulated. There are three principal ways of achieving interest:

Voicing – this refers especially to the note that is at the top of the chord. In some backings it can act as a simple melody in its own right. The chord progression

C Dm F G

could be voiced as follows:

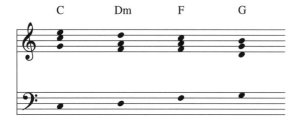

Rhythm – you don't have to play chords in a block at the start of each bar. A rhythmic pattern on a keyboard, or a strumming pattern on the guitar, will give life to the chords:

Figuration – the notes of the chords do not have to be played all at once, but can be spread:

EXERCISE ♪♪♪

A set of variations

Choose a chord progression (a four bar-one would be suitable) and devise a series of backing patterns either for guitar, bass or keyboard, each employing a different rhythm or figuration – like a set of variations. The example below is for bass guitar.

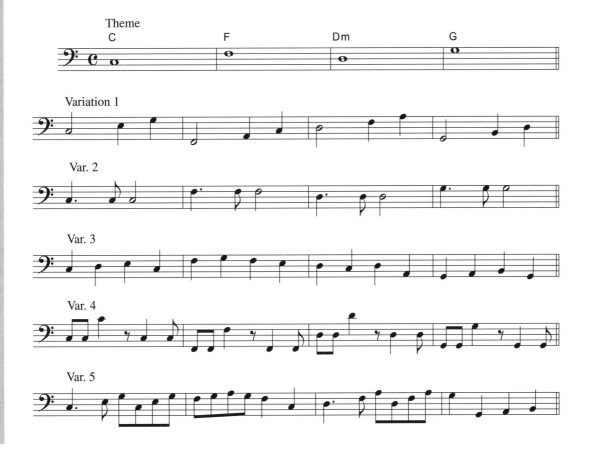

Two points to remember:

1 Make sure you don't write parts that are outside the range of the instrument.

2 When writing piano parts, don't forget that most of the singer-songwriters who perform at the piano were classically trained – Nina Simone, Neil Sedaka, Billy Joel, Elton John. Don't be afraid of using ideas drawn from classical pieces. Play and listen to sets of variations, sonatas and Romantic miniatures like studies and rhapsodies, especially those by the piano-playing composers like Mozart, Beethoven, Schumann and Chopin.

Percussion

We have looked at drums, but some bands also employ a separate percussion player (in addition to the kit drummer).

Latin percussion (see also Chapter 9) includes congas, bongos, timbales and a range of shakers (e.g. maracas and 'eggs' – the latter clear-sounding and cheap to buy), scrapers (guiros) and other hand-held items such as the cabasa and tambourine (though this is not strictly Latin American in origin). It may also include woodblocks, claves, cowbells and agogo bells (paired African bells).

An extra percussionist usually has a range of these instruments, plus cymbals. Obviously there is a limit to the number of parts that can be handled by one player, so if you want a complex Cuban or samba backing (see Chapters 9 and 11) you will need quite a few players.

Tuned percussion includes xylophone and marimba (like the xylophone but lower-pitched), and the metallic vibraphone and glockenspiel. It is quite common to use a synthesiser for these instruments, not only because these particular electronic timbres are passably good, but because the acoustic versions can be hard to mike up. One tuned instrument that *won't* need miking up is the timpani. This is occasionally heard in pop arrangements, for example Björk's *Human Behaviour*, where it provides as much punch as a bass drum, but with the added value of being tuned.

In addition, a range of percussion instruments can be brought into an arrangement for special purposes, for example if there is a world music influence. The African djembe drum is a wonderfully versatile instrument, as are the Indian tablas and the dhol (see Chapter 9). Producers and arrangers can be inventive: never underestimate the power of simple things: handclaps (e.g. the Beatles' *I want to hold your hand*), knee-slaps (Buddy Holly and the Crickets' *Everyday*, where the only drumming is Crickets drummer Jerry Allison slapping his hands on his knees), or triangle and scraper (Ben E King's *Stand by Me*).

PROJECT ♩♪ and ♩♪♪

Choose a song and make an unplugged arrangement for the class. Aim if possible at a five-part band – singer, acoustic guitar, piano, bass and percussion – but you may have to adapt this depending on the instruments available. For example, if there is no double bass you could use a cello playing pizzicato or rely on the left hand of the piano, or even a bass xylophone. Failing all else you may have to use an electronic keyboard timbre or a bass guitar.

Work out the chords first and arrange them for the backing instruments. Then add some simple percussion. Avoid a full drum kit and see what you can do with hand-held instruments: a tambourine, shaker or a clave on the offbeat.

Strings

In recent years real string instruments have gained in popularity over the string sound of the keyboard synthesiser. Most arrangements leave out the double bass (this role being covered by the bass guitar) and opt for a four-part string quartet texture: first and second violins, viola and cello.

There is an enormous difference between live strings and keyboard 'strings': most keyboard string parts are confined to block chords in the background and, because they are played by two hands, there is always a hole in the middle where the violas ought to be. Moreover, if the arrangement includes some independent parts they never convincingly replicate the effect of a bowed instrument.

Bowing is the key to good string writing. A down bow is strong, an up bow weaker, and the contrast between the two gives life to string writing. The phrase below can be bowed in a multitude of ways, all different, but here are a few options:

Down, up, down, up, down

All on a down bow

All on an up bow

Four notes down, one up

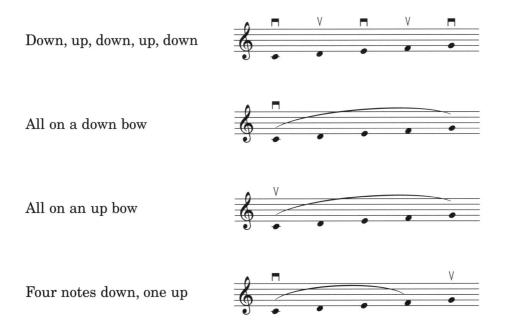

In addition to varieties of bowing, the strings can produce a wide range of effects, the best known being **pizzicato**, when the string is plucked with the finger rather than bowed. Also popular with arrangers is **portamento**, when the finger slides between one note and another to add expression. It is always worth asking string players to demonstrate different ways of playing a phrase.

String ensembles have been popular with bands. They have been used live by the Electric Light Orchestra (*Sweet Talking Woman*) and Oasis (*Don't Look Back in Anger*, *Champagne Supernova* and *Wonderwall*). Elvis Costello's *The Juliet Letters*, written for the Brodsky Quartet, was a fusion of popular song and classical chamber music.

LISTENING ♩♪

Two songs which feature a wide range of string effects:

She's Leaving Home (the Beatles)

A backing of strings and harp. There is a wide range of textures – sustained chords, detached chords, ostinati, flowing melodies, contrary motion in the parts. Note how the strings are woven around the vocals – sustained chords supporting the singer with 'fills' between the phrases.

Little L (Jamiroquai)

Here the strings take on a solo role and are bowed much more aggressively, almost imitating brass instruments. They play in unison for power, and to balance the rest of the band. Note the downward *glissandi* at the ends of the phrases.

Questions

In what ways are the approaches to string writing different?

Are the strings playing backing chords or melody?

Woodwind

Woodwind instruments tend to be used for solo work, the flute being a particular favourite. A woodwind ensemble is used very effectively on the 1997 arrangement of Elton John's *Candle in the Wind*, released to commemorate the funeral of Diana, Princess of Wales, and also in film composer Michael Kamen's orchestral collaboration with the heavy metal band Metallica, *S & M*, which features most of the instruments of the orchestra including a triple woodwind section.

EXERCISE ♪♪♪♪

Write a countermelody for a string or woodwind instrument to go with a vocal part. Start by working out the underlying harmonies, then add some instrumental fills to go in between the phrases, so that your countermelody doesn't intrude on the lyrics.

Brass and saxophones

The basic saxophone family consists of soprano, alto, tenor and baritone.

The basic brass family consists of trumpet, trombone, horn (also known as French horn) and tuba.

The saxophones are reed instruments, closely related to the clarinet, although (in pop music and jazz especially) they are often lumped together with the brass and referred to as 'the horns'. As a solo instrument the sax has been compared with the human voice and has been regularly used in a solo role. Examples include *Careless Whisper* (George Michael), *Brown Sugar* (Rolling Stones), *The Saxophone Song* (Kate Bush) and *The Logical Song* (Supertramp).

The brass and saxophones together (usually alto and tenor saxes, trumpet and trombone) are a powerful force in any line-up. They tend to give a big band feel to an arrangement, and are often associated with '60s soul songs such as those on the Tamla Motown and Atlantic labels, featuring artists like Marvin Gaye, the Four Tops and Aretha Franklin. Two examples of songs in this style with a 'horn' section of saxophones and brass are *The Tracks of My Tears* (the Miracles) and the soul-influenced Beatles song *Got to Get You Into My Life*. A large band was also used in the Tom Jones CD *Reload*.

Brass instruments can have a striking presence in an arrangement, especially the less commonly used ones, notable examples being the trumpet in D (higher pitched than the more usual trumpet in B♭) on *Penny Lane* (Beatles), the horn on *For No One* (Beatles), and the tuba on *Goodnight Ladies* (Lou Reed).

When arranging for a brass and saxophone section, try as a general rule to keep the upper parts close together. But leave a gap between these upper parts and the lowest one, since closely spaced intervals lower down will tend to make the chord sound muddy. The spacing should be like this:

The higher the instrument plays, the more powerful it becomes, but the part gets more difficult too, so always check whether your players can handle the high notes!

Backing Vocals

A chorus of backing singers originates in gospel, and is an ideal vehicle for any arrangement involving **call-and-response** effects (see page 26). Backing singers are also used to fill out an arrangement, either singing along with the lead or providing wordless 'ooohs' and 'aaahs' – as in *Arms of Mary* (Boyzone), which has a homophonic texture in the verses and backing 'ooohs' in the middle section.

An important distinction should be made between the **head voice**, a style of singing which is more choirboy-like, and the **chest voice**, which is more like shouting in tune. Some singers employ both – Minnie Ripperton had a huge vocal range, and Björk is able to switch her singing style very effectively. Male singers often use *falsetto* – high register – the best known example being the Bee Gees. Roy Orbison was renowned for his huge vocal range of almost three octaves.

FURTHER LISTENING

Midnight Train to Georgia (Gladys Knight and the Pips)
The lyrics are split between the lead singer and the backing group so as to form a dialogue. Sometimes one echoes the other, and sometimes the backing vocalists take over the main lyric, leaving Gladys Knight with an independent, semi-improvised part.

Could You Be Loved (Bob Marley)
Marley alternates with the backing vocalists to take a verse each.

You Can't Always Get What You Want (Rolling Stones)
A country ballad featuring the London Bach Choir. This develops into a very extravagant arrangement, the cultured vowels of the choir jarring ironically with Mick Jagger's mid-Atlantic drawl.

Church of the Poison Mind (Culture Club)
Boy George teams up with a powerful backing singer, Helen Terry, who belts out the verses. Her vocal gymnastics marry well with his gentler, more lyrical voice.

STUDY PROJECT ♪♪♪

How to arrange in four-part harmony

Being able to arrange a chord in four parts is an important skill, since it can be applied to wind, strings and vocals. It is easier if you follow these steps:

1 Write down the chords.

2 Work out the component notes.

3 Next, *either* write out the top line and the bass on a score:

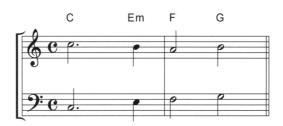

Or do it in table form:

chord	C	Em	F	G
top line	C	B	A	B
bass line	C	E	F	G

The bass notes should be the same as the root of the chord. Try to write something melodic in the top part, and avoid it hopping about.

4   Now add the inner parts. This is a four-part arrangement using three-note chords, so you will have to double one of the notes in each chord. Generally try to double the root or the fifth; double the third only if you have to.

Try to write flowing inner parts, and avoid them crossing over.

Check that what you've written can actually be played by the instruments you have in mind (i.e. that all the notes are within range).

chord	C	Em	F	G
top line	C	B	A	B
	G	G	F	G
	E	E	C	D
bass line	C	E	F	G

5   Once you have laid out the chords, think about the rhythm. In an up-tempo song don't be afraid to be bold. Vocals can employ quite explosive sounds derived from **scat** singing, whilst good brass players are capable of very quick articulation:

The computer

For many contemporary musicians, their instrument is the computer. Let's start by explaining some basic music technology terms.

MIDI

A system for connecting electronic instruments together. A MIDI keyboard is one in which the action of the keys can be sent to another keyboard as a set of signals via a MIDI cable. This allows remote control over the other keyboard. A sequencing program on a computer can record MIDI signals and play them back as an automated performance. It is important to understand that a MIDI signal does not contain the *sound* of the music – only a detailed numerical representation of the performance.

Audio

Sound converted into an electrical signal that can be heard over a loudspeaker.

WAV file

Sound converted into digital data. A WAV file cannot be played directly on a hi-fi but must first be loaded into a suitable computer program like Sound Forge or Audition, rather in the same way as a document file must opened in a word processing program before you can read it.

Digital

Digital sound is a system for converting sound into a series of electronic 'snapshots'. Because of the speed of the snapshots (usually 44,100 a second) the result might be compared to a cartoon in which the individual pictures all run together to produce continuous motion.

Analogue

A system of converting sound into a continuous electrical signal (as distinct from a succession of *digital* snapshots).

Sample

A digitally-recorded sound. Usually refers to a short phrase or drum pattern taken from an existing recording. Samples can be purchased as CD libraries (with the samples both in WAV and audio format) or they can be downloaded from the internet.

The sound card on even the most basic family computer will contain a bank of 128 MIDI timbres (different instrumental sounds) and will allow you to play WAV files. A more sophisticated sound card will allow you to do more, and will also be more efficient at processing the data. The MIDI timbres will conform to the General MIDI standard – an agreement reached by manufacturers to ensure that sound cards and other MIDI devices are standardised and compatible.

The 128 General MIDI (GM) sounds are grouped in families of instruments, eight at a time (so, for example, there are eight different types of piano). Each sound has its own individual number:

1–8	Pianos	65–72	Reeds
9–16	Tuned percussion	73–80	Flutes
17–24	Organs and accordion	81–88	Synth lead
25–37	Guitars	89–96	Synth pads
33–40	Bass instruments	97–104	Effects pads
41–48	Strings, timpani and harp	105–112	World music
49–56	Synth strings and choirs	113–120	Misc. percussion
57–64	Brass	121–128	Sound effects

In addition there is a full range of drum and percussion sounds, one for every note of the keyboard. Drum kit sounds are included on the lower half of the keyboard with Latin percussion in the upper half. Conveniently the sounds of the basic drum kit are all contained amongst the bottom few notes, so you should be able to find them easily.

There is a wide range of programs on the market which will enable you to link a keyboard to the computer and compose, Cubase and Logic being two of the most popular, although Ableton Live is growing in popularity. The keyboard can be connected via an **interface** cable (which connects directly to the sound card) or to the USB or firewire ports via an interface box. All that is needed to complete the workstation is a pair of loudspeakers and something to record the finished result on – or you can burn it onto the computer's CD writer.

The program allows you to compile MIDI tracks, using start/stop/record controls like a tape recorder to record and **overdub** the parts on the keyboard in time with a click track. They can be played back, and you can cut, copy and paste tracks or sections of tracks. There are also a number of editing displays where you can make fine adjustments, including a score editor which will allow you to prepare the music for printing (see page 76). One important function is **quantising**. This allows you to correct small rhythmic errors in your playing. For example, if you are not quite on the beat, the computer corrects this by moving all the notes you have played onto the beat. Care must be taken with this function, however, since music which is heavily quantised tends to sound very mechanical.

Timbres are selected on the track display; each track has its own set of controls with which you can select the timbre (just enter the GM number of the one you want) and control other features like volume, transposition and recording effects.

Each track is assigned to a **MIDI channel**, of which there are sixteen. In practice this imposes a limitation on the number of timbres you can select. If you have selected a piano sound on track 1, and if track 1 is assigned to MIDI channel 1, then any other track you assign to channel 1 will also play that piano sound. If you change the sound on track 1 to a bass guitar then all the other tracks on channel 1 will play bass guitar.

Usually the track number is the same as the channel number – track 1, channel 1; track 2, channel 2 and so on – but you can change the channel numbers. It is important to keep a note of what sounds you have assigned and which channel they are on. If you are attempting an orchestral arrangement it is surprising how quickly you run out of channels, even though you can have 64 or more tracks.

By agreement between manufacturers, the drum and percussion sounds are all on channel 10. It is usual to have several tracks on this channel, so you can keep the percussion parts separate and balance them independently – bass, snare and hi-hat on separate tracks, and cymbals and tom-toms on another.

Unless you spend a lot of money on a sound card, you may find some of the timbres disappointing compared with those on a commercial recording. If you can't afford more expensive equipment, there are a few ways round this problem. You can mix timbres by putting more than one on the same part (make copies of the original track and assign each one to a different MIDI channel – try harp, strings and a synth pad), or you can connect the computer via a MIDI cable to a keyboard or **sound module** and play the sounds on that instead of the computer (so long as you match the MIDI channels on the keyboard to the ones on the computer it should work).

You can also thicken up parts by copying them and editing the second one (for example a second bass part an octave below the first, or two string parts with one slightly delayed). Always listen to the results. Bear in mind that the number of tracks will be limited by another factor, the **polyphony**. This determines how many notes the card can play at any one time – if you exceed this, parts will be cut out.

MIDI can also be used to record tempo changes, and other performance details like changes of timbre, pedalling and effects. How much you can achieve with these **control messages** varies from one sound card to another.

Desktop studio programs such as these will also include a set of audio tracks alongside the MIDI ones – usually eight, but you can add more. These will allow you to record sound directly, either via a microphone, or from an instrument connected to the sound card, or from a CD player. The resulting track can be cut and pasted in the same way as a MIDI one. Also, you can **import** WAV files, for example a drum loop from a CD of samples.

Some programs are for audio only, including Audition, Sound Forge, Nuendo and WaveLab. These are effectively desktop recorders and editors, and the scope for music processing is usually very sophisticated. As in the MIDI programs above, the display is arranged in tracks which can be cut and pasted.

Projects for computer are included in Chapters 1 and 10.

CHAPTER 6

Production

The end product for most pop compositions is a recording, and this is usually the result of teamwork: a composer, a lyricist, a producer, and an engineer. The producer's job is to manage the entire recording process, often arranging the music and deciding how it will be recorded. The engineer runs the studio and operates the equipment. Sometimes a specialist arranger will be brought in, especially if a large ensemble of orchestral instruments or a big band is involved.

There are several ways of recording a song and all are possible under school conditions – but first, a note about the techniques and recording hardware.

Microphones

Basically, there are two types of microphone.

A **condenser** microphone is operated electronically and needs its own power supply. This can come from an internal battery – in which case it is called an **electret** microphone – or it can get its power from the mixing desk (see below) via the microphone lead. This type of power is called **phantom power**, and you would need to check that your mixing desk is able to supply this. The condenser microphone is sensitive, and is used for recording vocals and live acoustic instruments.

A **dynamic** microphone works mechanically and is more robust. It is less sensitive and is used to mike up loud instruments like drums, and for **close miking** amplifiers (see below).

In addition, microphones are categorised by the directions from which they pick up the sound. An **omni-directional** microphone operates like the human ear, picking up sound from all around, including the reflections and echoes from the walls as well as from the source itself.

A **cardioid** microphone is more focused, picking up most of the sound from the direction in which it is pointing. This means it records mainly the source, with only a small amount from the surroundings. Generally this type of microphone gives you more control, but it is susceptible to **proximity effect** – as it gets closer to the instrument, the sound becomes increasingly bass-heavy and unnatural. Some microphones are designed to overcome this, but if your budget is limited it is better to buy good general-purpose cardioids.

Microphone recording

Some of the best results in the classroom can be obtained relatively cheaply with a MiniDisc recorder and a stereo microphone. This is, in effect, two microphones in one, set up to point left and right and capture the sound in the room. An added advantage is that they are usually of the electret type, and come self-contained with their own battery.

An alternative is the so-called **crossed pair**: two cardioid condenser mikes on a stand at 90–120° to each other (the angle depending on how much 'spread' you want). These microphones are then connected to a mixing desk or recording device.

Both these arrangements work well for recording acoustic ensembles or singers with a guitar or piano. The best place for the microphones is usually arrived at through trial and error; get as close as you can to what you consider to be the 'best seat' in the audience and mount them above that.

Close miking

Here, a cardioid microphone is positioned close, so that it isolates the sound source. If you are recording live, then each instrument or voice will have to have its own microphone, and the result will be mixed at the mixing desk. A recording in which the parts are built up one at a time by overdubbing (see below) will require fewer microphones.

Miking up a band

Singers are best recorded with a cardioid condenser mike. They should be discouraged from holding the microphone and moving about as they may have seen live performers do. The best position for the microphone is about a foot away from, and level with, the singer's face. If there is a problem with **popping** – an explosive p-sound – then fit a **pop shield**. If there is a problem with sibilants – an unnaturally prominent 's' sound – then try a dynamic mike. The same positioning will usually work for solo wind players.

Acoustic guitars and pianos are also best recorded close miked with a cardioid condenser mike. The mike needs to point at the sound hole on the guitar, as close as you can get without interfering with the player. Pianos are difficult to mike up, but you will probably need two microphones about two feet away, one pointing at the upper strings and one at the lower ones. You will have to experiment with this – if the sound is too thin you might try one mike over the strings and one underneath the piano.

If you intend to mike up an amplified instrument you will need to place a dynamic mike pointing close to the loudspeaker on its amplifier. Alternatively you can connect the instrument directly to the mixing desk (you may need to connect through a **DI box** to match the instrument to the desk). Bear in mind that this may leave the player without a means of hearing what they are playing, so they will need headphones or their own monitor speaker.

Drum machines and digital drums will connect directly to the mixing desk. A live drum kit can be miked up with a crossed pair of condenser mikes above the kit. It may be helpful to put the drummer in a separate room or booth. Close miking a kit will produce a clearer sound with more control, but will require at least seven microphones:

➤ Bass drum – dynamic mike (there are special mikes for bass drums) mounted inside the drum (you will have to remove the front skin). You may also have to devise muffles, or stuff the drum with a blanket, to get the sound you want.

➤ Snare drum – a cardioid dynamic mike pointing at the edge of the skin about an inch away. Make sure it can't be hit by the drummer.

➤ Hi-hat – a cardioid condenser mike pointing down at the edge of the top cymbal. Make sure the cymbal doesn't hit the mike when it's lifted, and check that the mike is not picking up too much sound from the snare drum next to it.

➤ Top cymbals – overhead cardioid condenser mikes. You will probably need two. Position them about two feet away to start with, but always check the sound.

➤ Tom-toms – one dynamic mike per pair of drums, placed between them and pointing downwards to the skins. If there is no bottom skin, some engineers prefer to place the mike below, pointing upwards into the drum.

Always check the sound. School classrooms are not ideal for recording music with a microphone because there are so many hard, reflective surfaces. A room with carpets and curtains will provide a 'deader' ambience. Sometimes it is possible to improvise non-reflective shrouds by hanging blankets or attaching sheets of corrugated cardboard.

Making the recording

Live recording means just that, recording all the performers in one take. A simple stereo recording with a stereo mike or a crossed pair will produce good results with most acoustic performances, even one with a couple of individually amplified instruments, but the results will be poor for a fully amplified band.

If you have a selection of microphones and a mixing desk you could try **spot miking** – individually miking the key players (the singer would be an obvious choice for a spot mike). Extra microphones can be put to good use as **ambient mikes** – placed at the back of the room to collect some of the natural reverberation, adding depth and realism.

With a bigger mixing desk you might be able to close-mike everyone, and this will give you great control over the final sound. Whatever system you choose, you will probably be recording straight to stereo, so if you want to add effects (see below) this will have to be done at the same time.

How many tracks?

First let's be clear about the difference between **tracks** and **channels**:

Track	A stereo recording is **two-track** (left and right). A multitrack recorder can have anything from four tracks upwards. It is possible to record several instrumental parts on a single track, but only if they are all recorded at the same time. If you want to record them separately you will have to record each on its own track. (Confusingly, the separate songs on a recorded album are also called 'tracks', but that's a quite different use of the word: they are played one after the other, not at the same time.)
Channel	This has two meanings:
	a) In MIDI it refers to the system by which instrumental timbres are selected.
	b) On a mixing desk it refers to the number of individually controlled inputs. For example, a sixteen-channel desk can have sixteen microphones or instruments plugged into it, each with its own volume fader and effects controls. The channels can be routed to the tracks of the recording device in almost any combination.

With a multitrack recorder you will gain more control, since you will be able to assign instruments to their own track and mix them together later. How many tracks you can use will depend on the number of channels on your mixing desk and, crucially, on the number of tracks on your multitrack recorder.

In a professional studio the engineer will use a multitrack recording program on the computer, and the set-up will consist of either a mixing desk connected directly to the computer sound card or everything being controlled at the computer with an on-screen mixing desk. As an alternative, some studios use a multitrack digital recorder (the eight-track ADAT is popular), or even a reel-to-reel multitrack tape recorder.

Still common in schools is the **portastudio**. This is a combined mixing desk and multi-track recorder (usually four or eight tracks) which can be either digital, MiniDisc or a cassette tape. The digital ones are relatively inexpensive, easy to use and give clear recordings, but they may not have enough memory for an entire school concert.

Overdubbing

A multitrack recorder (or computer program) will allow you to record one part at a time, building up to the final performance. The multitrack facility allows the player to hear what has already been recorded and to record their own part over the top.

It is customary to start with the drums, the drummer playing the part in time with a pre-recorded click track, or with a guide track (perhaps the composer strumming through the chords of the song). Next comes the bass, and then the rhythm parts. Once these **backing tracks** are complete, the vocals and solos are added last.

There are many advantages to this technique. It requires fewer microphones and fewer players; in theory a single player can record *all* the parts. It also allows control over the process. If someone makes a mistake you only have to re-record that part (it is even possible to **drop in** and replace just the offending section).

Most importantly, a multitrack recording will result in a **master**, which will then have to be **mixed down** in what is called the **post-production** process. Here, the mixing desk is used to arrive at a final balance, including any effects, and to reduce everything to a stereo mix for the final recording. It is common to make this final recording onto a computer and then to burn a CD, but the alternatives are to record onto MiniDisc or cassette tape.

The computer backing track

Here, much of the arrangement is prepared on the computer. The procedure is much the same as for any multitrack recording. The tracks can consist of MIDI parts or samples – for example the drum patterns – or a combination of both.

The advantage of working at the computer is that it gives you plenty of time to make decisions. The disadvantage is that you may be tied to the MIDI sounds available on the sound card.

When you have completed the backing it is possible to record the vocal part directly onto an audio track, but bear in mind that the vocalist will need to be able to hear the backing (through a pair of headphones). On some computers there can be an unnerving time delay between the actual sound and the one that comes out of the computer, an effect called **latency**. One solution is to record the backing onto a multitrack recorder as described above, and then overdub additional parts such as the vocals. If you have an audio editing program you can record the backing mix onto that, and then add the vocals. The latency may not be so bad when you are no longer trying to combine MIDI and audio. Alternatively you can try a 'live' mix, playing the computer and recording the voice at the same time onto a tape or MiniDisc. The best solution, however, is to invest in an **interface**. This connects the singer's microphone to the computer via a USB or firewire port and allows you to record MIDI, vocals and instruments, turning your computer into a multitrack recorder and giving you more control over the number of tracks you can record.

Post production

When recording instruments it is customary to record them **flat** – that is, without any effects or processes (apart from the guitar, whose effects are integral to its sound). Effects are best added at the mixing down stage, when you have some control over them. Remember that effects, once recorded, cannot be removed.

The most common effects are:

Panning   The pan control is found on the mixing desk, and determines which side of the stereo mix the sound will come from, left or right. Each channel has its own pan control, one of several controls arranged in a column above the fader for that channel.

It is possible to 'position' the various instruments. When panning, try to be realistic, using the faders to help: the singer and drums should both be in the middle, but the singer should be audible above the drums. The lead guitar could be slightly to the right and the rhythm guitar slightly to the left.

Equalisation   The **EQ** controls are also found on the mixing desk, one set for each channel. In essence they are tone controls. Usually there are at least two – treble and bass – but the more expensive mixing desks have a **mid-range** one as well. Moving the control anticlockwise will reduce that frequency-range, and moving it clockwise will boost it. The EQs are used to enhance the colour of an instrument, for example brightening up the cymbals or adding some depth to the bass. Boosting the mid-range and cutting the treble and bass will create a cheap loudspeaker effect, making the recording sound old-fashioned – an effect which some artists, such as Moby and Eminem, have exploited.

The effects described above are an integral part of the mixing desk. Others are created by special effects units which must be purchased separately and connected to the desk via an **effect send** socket.

Reverberation   Reverberation ('reverb') is the natural liveliness of a space, caused by sound reflecting off the walls and surfaces. It is not to be confused with echo (or **delay**), which is an exact repetition of the original sound bouncing back.

Reverb gives depth to a performance (this is why people think they sing better in the bath) and can also be used to create the illusion of distance (the greater the reverb the further away the sound will appear to be). Most effects processors have a range of reverb types whose names are self-explanatory: dark hall, large room, etc.

Delay   This is an artificial echo. A very short echo (less than half a second) will tend to 'fatten' up the sound, whilst a longer echo will give the illusion of space, especially when combined with reverberation.

Compression   A compressor is a device that limits the volume. When applied to a vocal track it prevents the singer's voice from distorting the recording when it gets loud, for example on a high note. Compression is fundamental to the production of popular music, which (unlike classical music) always tends to remain at the same level on a recording. However, using a compressor effectively is an art form in itself.

Having tried and tested all the possibilities, it is time to record the final stereo version. One last comment: whether recording an individual instrument or mixing down an entire performance, always check and recheck the recording levels. That is what the meters are for. Ideally the sound should be peaking just into the red.

PROJECT ♪♪♪ and ♪♪♪♪

Building a backing track

This project is best undertaken by making a cover version of a song. That way, the additional task of having to compose all the material is avoided. It also assumes that the final performance will be sung, but the tasks can apply equally to an instrumental.

1   Start by acquainting yourself with the structure. If you can work alongside the singer, that will help the project. Remember that this is a backing track to support someone's performance. You will have to take account of their needs. Which key would be best? What tempo and feel are they comfortable with? How many choruses will there be, and how should they be paced? Will there be a climax? How will the vocal part interact with instrumental solos?

2   Get the feel right. Devise a basic drum pattern for the various sections of the song: verses, choruses and middle. Then add the bass.

3   Go back over the drum part and work out the fills and any extra percussion.

4   Add the rhythm parts: guitars and keyboards. Keep a check on the texture – is there enough variety?

5   Now go back over the drums again and add punctuation (small-detail cymbal crashes and accents for subtlety).

6   Now think again about the overall structure, the order of verses, choruses, middles and solos. Will there be an introduction? (Find out what the singer wants!) Will there be a coda?

7   At this point you might start to add brass or strings (if there are to be any) and to think about instrumental solos. If these are going to be woven around the lead singer's part then you can leave them until this has been recorded, but if they have already been worked out and rehearsed then they could be recorded now. The singer may prefer to work with them in the backing track.

It can be hard to find opportunities to work as a producer/engineer, so make use of any songs you can find in the classroom which are already in multitrack form. Ask the composer's permission if you can have a go at remixing their song. Remix last year's student work. Record the school concert. Record a classroom performance by another year group.

Scoring parts

Written-out parts are unusual in popular music – most musicians prefer to rely on memory, and much popular music is improvised or composed by musicians who do not read music. However, it is sometimes helpful to write the music down, and this is a requirement for some examinations. There is not space to cover the details of notation, editing and printing in this book, but the reader is directed to Daryl Runswick's excellent *Rock, Jazz and Pop Arranging* (Faber Music, 1993).

A fully notated part is rare – these are confined to the big shows where everything is scored by an arranger and where the practice of 'depping' (standing in for the regular player at short notice) means that a clear, comprehensive part is essential.

Some bands make do with a simple list of chords and the order of the verses and choruses – for instance:

Verse	C F C Bdim E Am F G C
Chorus	C G Am F
V1 V2 C V3 M C (repeat)	

More common is the **chord chart**. A chart can be produced as a simple table (see page 45):

								1 *Fine*	2	
‖: C	Em	F	G	C	F Dm	G	C :‖		E	

D.C. al Fine

Am	G	F	G	Am	F	Dm7	G7

Alternatively, a chart can be written on a conventional stave. The advantage of a five-line stave is that details, such as important riffs and drum patterns, can be notated at critical points.

Published songs often take the form of a **lead sheet**, in which the vocal line is written out with lyrics and with chord symbols above the stave, or a **song sheet**, which is the same but with an added piano arrangement.

Most computer programmes will allow you to print scores and parts, and some do this more easily than others. **Sibelius** is an industry-standard printing package, and will allow you to produce work to publishing standard. However, it is not a sophisticated recording production tool, so if you are intending to make a recording as well as a score, you would be advised to prepare each on a separate program. If you are composing with MIDI you can transfer ideas between two programs by saving the work as a **MIDI file**, but bear in mind that samples will not be notated automatically. There is software that will convert audio into notation, but it is quite tricky to use. If you are preparing a full score which includes sampled material then this can be sketched in outline on one of the parts.

Always try to provide some detail for the players. If you can include tempo, dynamics, accents and phrasing – and particularly rehearsal letters – this will save time in rehearsal.

Scores and parts can be printed off music production software, but you will have to do some editing before it will be presentable. The problem with MIDI software is that it notates exactly what you play – so if you are a fraction behind the beat the music will be notated a fraction behind the beat, and will be unreadable. This can be overcome by **quantising** the score (this function is explained on page 68). This moves all the notes you have played onto a beat, so they can be read clearly. You can also remove or reduce ledger lines by adding an appropriate clef, and likewise reduce accidentals by adding a key signature. It is possible for a non-reading musician to print off a passable score by following the basic instructions, but the result may lack subtlety.

Answers
to listening exercises

Listening exercise, page 47

Identifying the chords

Rockin' all over the world (Status Quo)

|I | |IV | |I |V |I | ||

Heartbreak Hotel (Elvis Presley)

|I | | | |IV | |V |I ||

Fun, Fun, Fun (Beach Boys)

|I | |IV | |I | |V | | |

|I | |IV | |I   V |IV V |I   V |IV V ||

Listening exercise, page 55

Identifying the instruments

God Only Knows (Beach Boys)

Horn, piano, bass guitar, tambourine, woodblock, backing vocals, strings (pizzicato), snare drum, synthesiser

Isobel (Björk)

Strings, trumpet, tom-toms, snare drum, synth bass, synthesiser, woodblock, cymbal, flute, backing vocals, human whistling

PART 2

Topics

CHAPTER 7

Riffs

Riffs play an important role in popular music. A riff is a short repeated phrase, usually lasting one or two bars. It can be repeated continuously or with gaps in between, and it can be played in the bass or as a lead or rhythm part.

The use of riffs dates back to early blues where a whole song might be performed over a single repeated riff. Examples of this are:

Hoochie Coochie Man	Muddy Waters
Smokestack Lightnin'	Howlin' Wolf

Some of the most famous songs in the history of pop feature riffs. Here are some more examples:

Twist and Shout	The Beatles
Pretty Woman	Roy Orbison
You Really Got Me	The Kinks
Whole Lotta Love	Led Zeppelin
The Jean Genie	David Bowie
Superstition	Stevie Wonder
Bad	Michael Jackson
Start Me Up	Rolling Stones
Sign of the Times	Prince
One Vision	Queen
To Cut a Long Story Short	Spandau Ballet
Know Your Enemy	Rage Against the Machine
Fun Lovin' Criminals	Fun Lovin' Criminals
Give it Away	Red Hot Chilli Peppers
Tell Her Tonight	Franz Ferdinand

There are two elements to a memorable riff: melody and rhythm.

Sometimes it is helpful to start with the rhythm. Chapter 1 includes some exercises for devising rhythmic patterns.

Riff melodies are usually quite simple, rarely consisting of more than five different notes, and sometimes using just two. The notes are often drawn from a pentatonic (five-note) scale such as the one shown below:

Riffs can also be based on other scales. This example uses the first five notes of the major scale:

And they can, of course, be played as a bass line.

LESSON PLAN ♪ and ♪♪

Building a riff

Equipment Keyboards

Task Working in pairs, compose a riff using the notes of this pentatonic scale:

Start simply with a riff on two pitches, for instance:

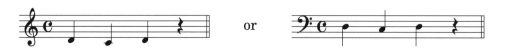

Don't forget that you can repeat notes:

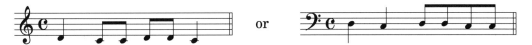

Then try using more pitches:

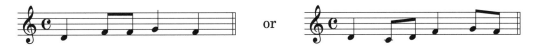

Sometimes riffs work better if you include rests:

Help
If you get stuck, try tapping the rhythm first, then playing it on a single pitch, then changing some of the pitches. Or get your partner to clap a rhythm to which you add notes.

Development
Compose three contrasting riffs and use them to compile a 16-bar phrase. This one is in the bass. (The sign in bar 2 means 'repeat the previous bar'.)

The form of the one above is ABCA. Try other patterns:

AABA   ABBA   ABAC

Devise a riff and transpose it up and down in line with the root of the chord:

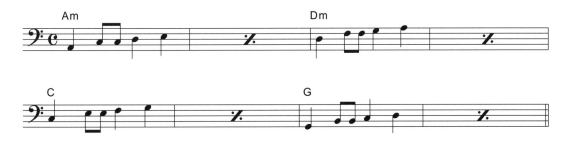

LESSON PLAN ♪

Composing a rap

Equipment	Keyboards, newspapers, comics, magazines, scissors, paper, glue, pens
Task	Working in small groups, compose and perform a short rap over a repeated riff.
Listening	For a rap based on a guitar riff, listen to *Give it Away* (Red Hot Chilli Peppers).
	For a rap based on a synthesised riff and a drum machine listen to *The Real Slim Shady* (Eminem).
Process	A quick way to write a set of lyrics is to cut out slogans, phrases and captions from newsprint or a comic. These can be stuck onto a card and the words copied out as needed (or they can be word-processed and then printed).
	Practise rapping the words to a pulse, then devise a riff (or riffs) to go with them as a backing.
	Don't forget to try the riff at a different octave (i.e. starting higher up or lower down the keyboard) – it might work better as a bass line.
Help	If your keyboard has a drum machine, you may find this helpful for keeping in time.
Development	Extend the rap into a structure with verses and a chorus:

       verse   chorus   verse   chorus   chorus

Try adding some percussion.

To the teacher

To save time, groups could be given pre-prepared flash cards with the words already cut out and pasted.

WORKSHEET ♪♪♪

This is based on a GCSE listening paper. The questions relate to the David Bowie song *The Jean Genie*, but the format of the questions could be adapted to any riff-based song.

Play the song up to the end of the first chorus, twice. Then repeat as often as required.

Questions

1. How many different pitches are there in the riff?

2. How many times is the whole riff heard before the chorus begins?

3. Which of the three diagrams below most closely follows the melodic shape of the riff?

    a)

    b)

    c)

4. Which of the three bars below shows the correct rhythm of the riff?

Adding a new section

A continuously repeated riff can give a very hypnotic effect to a song, but songwriters often break the pattern and introduce contrasting sections. Here are some examples:

Bo Diddley (Bo Diddley)
The riff is a guitar pattern, strummed to a *clave* rhythm (see page 10). This is one of the basic rhythmic patterns of Latin America and can be heard in many examples of samba, latino, and in the backing parts of much club dance music (see Chapters 9 and 11). In *Bo Diddley* the riff is played almost continuously except for a short two-chord break.

Jumping Jack Flash (Rolling Stones)
The verse is sung over a two-bar guitar riff. At the chorus the backing changes to one chord per bar, a change of harmonic rhythm which gives the song tremendous energy.

Whole Lotta Love (Led Zeppelin)
A classic riff from a song which for many years was the opening music of the BBC programme *Top of the Pops*. The riff has three bars of repeated power chords on the guitar followed by a short phrase in the fourth bar, and continues throughout the song apart from an improvised middle section for voice and drums. Its return is a dramatic high point in the performance.

Another One Bites the Dust (Queen)
Another classic riff – this one for bass guitar. The riff is in two parts – a repeated note followed by a phrase (a similar structure to *Whole Lotta Love*), and this is used to accompany the verses. There is a contrasting section which feels like an interlude. (Compare this with the next example by Michael Jackson, in which the contrasting section is a chorus.)

Bad (Michael Jackson)
As in *Another One Bites the Dust* the riff is in the bass (but here played by a keyboard synthesiser). The riff is in two parts, bar 2 being a variant of bar 1. The riff accompanies the verse, pauses during the bridge, then powerfully comes back in for the chorus.

WORKSHEET ♩♪

Play *Another One Bites the Dust* and *Bad* up to the end of their first choruses.

Questions

1. In both songs the riff is in the bass. In what ways are the instruments different?

2. In both songs the riff is two bars long.

    In which song does the riff start with repeated notes?

    Which song has the riff with the greatest number of different pitches?

    Which song has a chorus?

Compose a riff-based instrumental with a four-bar break

If you are using a keyboard (or have a drum machine or drum samples) it may help if you choose a drum pattern to work in time to.

Compose a two-bar riff. Play four times to create a verse 8 bars long.

Compose a four-bar break to follow your 8 bars. This could be any of the following:

    a new two-bar riff, played twice

    a new one-bar riff, played four times

    a chord pattern, either one chord per bar or one chord every two bars

You should end up with a 12-bar structure like this. (The sign going across the barline in bars 3–4 means 'repeat the previous two bars'.)

Play it through. You may find it balances better if you repeat the four-bar break.

Now try playing the whole thing through twice.

What does the song need now? A middle section? Turn back to Chapter 4 for ideas about structure.

Tubular Bells

Tubular Bells is an extended instrumental piece written in 1973 by Mike Oldfield. Its huge sales helped to establish Virgin as a major record label (which subsequently grew into the Virgin business empire). Oldfield, a highly skilled guitarist and multi-instrumentalist, recorded the parts himself, overdubbing many times to build complex textures in a composition lasting nearly fifty minutes. The music consists of riffs and melodies woven together, which is why it is featured in this chapter.

Some writers have called it a rock symphony, but it is not strictly speaking symphonic; the ideas do not really develop as you might expect them to do in a symphony, and it rarely moves far from the home key of A minor. However, it is in contrasting sections and each half ends in the dominant (E major), which provides for a sense of climax and tonal uplift. The device of ending triumphantly in the major has been employed by many classical composers, the best known example perhaps being Beethoven's Fifth Symphony, which shifts to the tonic major key for its last movement.

Other writers have drawn attention to the fact that many of the techniques of *Tubular Bells* are similar to those of minimalism. Minimalism was quite new in 1973, and Oldfield is known to have heard early examples including Terry Riley's *Rainbow in Curved Air*. However, when interviewed about the piece he has not attached much importance to minimalism, saying that he was more interested in the melodies than the repeated riff patterns. It is more likely that he was influenced by albums like Santana's *Abraxas* (1970), on which there is a great deal of solo guitar work and songs backed by riffs and rhythmic patterns.

Structure

The piece is in two halves, originally recorded on two sides of a vinyl LP, but now issued as two tracks on a CD. Each opens in A minor with a series of melodies built over a repeated riff and climaxing with a melody in the major key.

Tonality and harmony

The overall tonal plan is as follows:

Part 1   A minor, F♯ major, B major, A minor, F♯ major, A minor, E minor, E major

Part 2   A minor, E minor, A minor, E major

The chord progressions are generally quite simple: four-, eight- and twelve-bar repeated patterns which support many melodic parts (rather like a round). There are no modulations as such, but transitions in which the harmony moves either round the cycle of fifths or in semitones to the destination key. For example, the route from A minor to E major, might take this form:

Am, Dm, D♭, C, B, E

Melody

Oldfield drew on a wide repertoire of styles. Part 1 includes two melodies which are quite romantic in feel, while Part 2 has a medley of folk tunes, a heavy-metal riff and concludes with a hornpipe.

Metre and rhythm

Variety is achieved through changes in metre and tempo. Two of the most important riffs are constructed using a tight rhythmic plan. The treble riff which opens Part 1 is based on a pattern – rather like a *tala* – of thirty quavers grouped in bars as follows:

$$\frac{7}{8} \quad \frac{7}{8} \quad \frac{7}{8} \quad \frac{9}{8}$$

The bass riff which opens Part 2 is repeated unvaried but combined with a series of melodies, the inner parts consisting of phrases of unequal length, so that as they are repeated they coincide at different points (a device which is sometimes called 'phasing' and is a common feature of minimalist music).

Timbre

Oldfield is fond of repeating a melody on a succession of different instruments. This is most obvious at the close of Part 1, where the texture builds and where each new instrument playing the main theme is announced by a speaker on the recording.

There is a performance project for the whole class based on combined riffs in Chapter 11.

CHAPTER 8

Songs

This chapter consists of analyses of selected songs by composers dating from the 1920s to the present day:

George Gershwin
Burt Bacharach
Lennon and McCartney
Stevie Wonder
Bob Marley
Michael Jackson
Elton John

Recordings of the songs featured are all easily available, along with the sheet music, and could form the basis of a performance project or a history and analysis unit. The text assumes some musical vocabulary and a familiarity with the study of set works. Each song is broken down into its musical elements, for example melody, harmony, structure – which is how most exam questions are framed. The analyses have drawn on current recordings and publications, but some schools may have song sheets and arrangements that differ in detail. Rather than being a disadvantage, it may prove a useful exercise to spot the differences.

GEORGE GERSHWIN (1896–1937)

Gershwin is a pioneering figure in popular music history. He was a staff pianist for the New York publishers Remick, and was one of the first songwriters to achieve world fame (beginning with the success of *Swanee* in 1920). Many of his songs have become jazz 'standards'. His principal successes belong to the late 1920s and 1930s, when he combined work in Hollywood with work for the concert hall, developing a fusion of blues, jazz and classical music as exemplified in *Rhapsody in Blue* and the opera *Porgy and Bess*.

The Man I Love (1924)

From the musical *Lady Be Good*

Structure

Four-bar instrumental introduction followed by a verse of two eight-bar phrases. The refrain, in 32-bar form, is sung twice through and contains the title line of the song. This structure is distantly related to the recitative and aria of opera, and was popular with songwriters in the 1920s and '30s, especially those composing for the musical theatre, when the introduction was usually a dramatic link into the song.

---

88 ◆ Part 2 Chapter 8

Harmony

The introduction opens in C minor and moves through a series of chromatic harmonies to the home key of E♭. The harmony of the verse is based around chords I, IV and V, briefly suggesting a move through the mediant minor during the second phrase.

The refrain is characterised by its blue notes – the flattened seventh on the word 'along' and the flattened fifth of the chord on the word 'way'.

The middle eight of the 32-bar refrain (starting at 'Maybe I shall meet him Sunday') is in the relative minor. Note the chromatically descending inner parts in the accompaniment.

Melody

Much of the melody is sequential, both in the verse (bars 1–2, 3–4 and 5–6) and in the refrain.

Summertime (1935)

From the opera *Porgy and Bess*

Structure

Strophic – two verses with an instrumental introduction and a short coda (which in the original opera was a link leading to the next item).

Harmony

The first part of the verse is built over a repeating two-chord pattern, bluesy in feel and adopted by many songwriters since. Here the chords are Bm(maj6) and C♯m(maj6). The first change, after four bars (at 'fish are jumpin' '), is to the subdominant, again a typical blues move.

Melody

The operatic original is pitched quite high, being intended for a classically trained singer, but the song is often performed by jazz singers who pitch it lower down, using a chest voice.

A Foggy Day (1937)

From the Fred Astaire film *A Damsel in Distress*

Structure

Four-bar instrumental introduction and 16-bar verse leading to a 32-bar refrain, but not in standard 32-bar form. This one is in two sections: a basic binary structure of ABAC in which the C phrase is extended to ten bars, making 8+8+8+10 bars in all.

The introduction is more recitative-like than in *The Man I Love*. It is in two eight-bar phrases: (4+4) + 8. The second phrase does not answer the first, but introduces new material sung over an A pedal with chromatic harmonies above.

Harmony

There is much of interest in this song. In the introduction, note:

➤ the opening bars for piano, depicting the chimes of Big Ben, harmonised in chords built in fourths

➤ the passing parallel chords harmonising the first line, 'I was a stranger in the city'

➤ passing modulations though mediant and supertonic minors

➤ change of harmonic rhythm (the pedal under 'as I walked through the foggy streets alone')

In the refrain:

➤ blue notes in the melody on 'day' and 'low'

➤ regular harmonic rhythm

Melody

This is one of Gershwin's finest. Much of it is built on the chimes of Big Ben and uses word painting to suggest bells: the opening piano bars, the first line ('I was a stranger in the city') with its bell-like scale, the chant-like setting of 'as I walked through the foggy streets alone' with its tolling bell effect over a pedal, and the bell-like motif of the last line of the refrain ('and through foggy London town...').

The refrain is typically sequential, but note how Gershwin alternates the melodic contours. The first four lines all end with an upward interval. These are answered by two phrases ending in a downward interval ('I viewed the morning...'). The singer hits the highest note at the climax of the refrain ('For suddenly I saw you there'), giving the effect of the fog lifting.

BURT BACHARACH

Burt Bacharach wrote hit songs for many of the major recording artists of the '60s and '70s, including Dionne Warwick and Dusty Springfield, and was one of the first song-writers to set the trend for releasing a successful hit single as part of the soundtrack of a feature film. Examples include *What's New Pussycat?*, *Alfie*, *Raindrops Keep Falling on my Head* (from *Butch Cassidy and the Sundance Kid*) and *Arthur's Theme* (for which he won an Oscar).

The Look of Love (1967)

Written for the film *Casino Royale* and recorded by Dusty Springfield

Structure

Similar to the AABA structure of the 32-bar song, but (typically for Bacharach) with a great deal of variation:

A   eight-bar phrase
A′ the first phrase repeated and extended to 10 bars

B   6-bar middle (but it feels like a chorus)
Repeat A, A′ and B′

Harmony

Bacharach tends to use quite basic harmonies, but they are often decorated by the addition of sevenths and suspensions, and he varies the harmonic rhythm. Here are the chords of the opening phrase:

Dm7sus | |Am7 | |B♭ |B♭6 |A7sus |A7 |

The middle is in the relative major, giving it the feel of a chorus. At the end of this section, the music jumps back to the minor key of the verse without any preparatory modulation.

Melody and rhythm

A special feature of Bacharach's melodies is the rhythm. The opening phrase is broken up into short two-note motifs:

Close to You (1963)

The best-known version is the one by the Carpenters.

Structure

32-bar song.

Harmony

An interesting song because the tonic and dominant harmonies are stated so infrequently. The verse opens on a subdominant ninth and the tonic chord is not stated until the cadence at the end of the first section (on the words 'close to you'). Likewise, the middle section opens in the subdominant and closes on the dominant (the only time the dominant chord is heard in the entire song).

Rhythm

Note how Bacharach adapts to the changes in accent in Hal David's lyric:

Why do **birds** suddenly ap-**pear**

Every **time** you are **near**?

Just like me **they** long to be

Close to you

JOHN LENNON AND PAUL McCARTNEY

Although the Beatles habitually referred to themselves as a rock'n'roll band, they broke new ground in popular music: they were among the first bands to write their own material, they introduced their audiences to new developments in rock and soul from the USA, and they developed new recording techniques with their producer George Martin.

Can't Buy Me Love (1964)

Structure

An unusual song because it takes its title from the words of the middle section, with the result that most listeners would feel this to be the chorus rather than the eight-bar middle it actually is. This title phrase is established early on as a hook: the song opens with a short introduction based on this section. The verses are a standard 12-bar blues.

Harmony

The middle/chorus is in the mediant minor, eight bars long, a simple chord sequence leading back to the verse:

| Am | Dm | F | F |
| Am | Dm | Gm7 | C7 |

Penny Lane (1967)

The 32-bar song was a popular form with the Beatles, and *Penny Lane* is interesting both for its arrangement, featuring a solo trumpet in D, and its harmony. The middle eight serves as a chorus; the words contain the title of the song (as well as its melodic hook) and are repeated. However, it is in quite a remote key and returns to the home dominant at the end, giving it the feel of a standard middle eight.

Structure

The song builds from a simple first eight bars to an increasingly complex arrangement.

A (verse)
A (verse with flute and drums)
B (chorus/middle with brass)
A (verse with flute and drums)
A (verse with trumpet solo)
B (chorus/middle with brass)
A (as opening verse, no drums)
A (verse with drums)
B (chorus/middle with trumpet countermelody)
B (up a tone with trumpet and piccolo countermelody)
Coda

Harmony

The eight-bar verse, in G major, starts with a simple bass line but rapidly passes through the relatively remote tonic minor on its way to the middle section, which is in F major. The return, via a dominant chord, is left until the very last bar.

Melody

Note how much of the melody consists of stepwise movement – also the similarity between the melody of the verse and that of the middle.

Step Inside Love (1968)

Never recorded by the Beatles, but written for Cilla Black: a ballad containing an extraordinary mixture of jazz and rock.

Structure

Verse and chorus. The verse, with a clear soft jazz feel, consists of an eight-bar phrase plus a six-bar phrase (overlapping the first bar of the chorus). The chorus, ten bars, has more of a rock feel.

Harmony

The jazz feel in the verse is partly the result of two tritone substitutions (see page 41) in bars 3–5 (Gm7, G♭7, F) and bars 7–9 (Fm7, E7, E♭).

The rock feel in the chorus is partly the result of the standard pentatonic rock chord sequence C, E♭, B♭, F.

Melody

Note how the phrases in the verse tend to end with a rising interval while those in the chorus tend to end with a falling one.

Come Together (1969)

Another unusual song. The chorus is very short and starts on a remote harmony.

Structure

Verse and chorus, highly contrasted. The verse is sung for the most part over a sparse backing of bass riff and drum fills, whilst the chorus is accompanied by guitar power chords. Both the four-bar introduction and the eight-bar verse are repeated before the four-bar chorus.

Harmony

Verse in C minor, chorus in A minor. The chordal structure is actually very simple, and depends for its impact on the switch from C minor to A minor and back again.

Verse	Cm7 (4 bars)	G7 (2 bars)	F7 (2 bars)
Chorus	Am F	G	Cm

Let It Be (1970)

This song, which has arguably achieved anthem status, proves that there is still mileage in the standard chord pattern I VI IV V.

Structure and instrumentation

Piano introduction. Verse and chorus. Note how the arrangement builds through the addition of simple backing vocals to the guitar solo in the middle.

> Introduction – piano
> Verse 1 – voice and piano
> Chorus with backing vocals and organ
> Verse 2 with simple cymbal echo pattern – bass added on repeat
> Chorus – heavier drum pattern with organ
> Chorus repeat with brass
> Bridge and instrumental verse 3 (guitar solo)
> Chorus with brass
> Verse 4 with maracas and guitar fill on repeat
> Chorus
> Chorus repeated with guitar overlay
> Coda – based on bridge

Harmony

Very simple, being a reordering of the same four chords.

> The verses consist of I V VI IV
> The choruses consist of VI V IV I

STEVIE WONDER

Since his debut as a child star with Tamla Motown in the early '60s Stevie Wonder has sustained his position as one of the most versatile and influential post-war songwriters.

My Cherie Amour (1968)

A simple ballad with a wordless chorus and the quality of a jazz standard.

Structure

> Introduction – same as the chorus: a four-bar phrase sung to la-la
> Verse 1
> Verse 2 – note backing strings
> Chorus
> Verse 3 – note backing strings
> Chorus – fade

Harmony and melody

The melodic line in the verses consists almost entirely of jazz dissonances on the strong beats:

	7th	**11th**	**7th**
My che -	rie amour _____	lovely as a summer	day
My che -	rie amour _____	distant as the milky	way
	7th	**13th**	**13th**
My che -	rie amour _____	pretty little one that	I adore
		5th	**9th**
		You're the only girl my	heart beats for
		6th	**root**
		How I wish that you were	mine

The phrases are also very economically structured, being based on two simple rhythmic motifs.

	rhythm 1	**rhythm 2**	
My che -	rie amour _____	lovely as a summer	day
My che -	rie amour _____	distant as the milky	way
(sequential repeat)			**rhythm 1**
My che -	rie amour _____	pretty little one that	I adore
		You're the only girl my	heart beats for
		How I wish that you were	mine

Superstition (1972)

The opening riff, one of the most famous in popular music, forms the accompaniment to this song, whose driving energy made it a forerunner of the disco craze of the late 1970s and, subsequently, Michael Jackson's later work and contemporary dance music.

Structure

Verses punctuated by a four-bar break – too short to be described as either a middle or a chorus.

Riffs, harmony and production

The verses are sung over a syncopated two-bar riff around the tonic harmony of C minor.

In the second half of the verse a countermelody is added, played in octaves by the brass.

The break consists of a four-bar chordal change around the dominant:

| G   A♭ | G   F♯dim | F | G |

Sir Duke (1976)

Stevie Wonder's tribute to Duke Ellington. The production uses quite a big band but, as in *Superstition*, he shows a fondness for economical textures: octaves for the saxophone and brass solos and a basic four-part combo for the verses.

Structure and instrumentation

> Verse (8 bars) – note simple four-part backing (guitar, bass, keyboard and drums)
> Bridge (8 bars)
> Chorus – with band
> Solo – band in octaves with drums

This is repeated. Note the siren and woodblocks in the second chorus.

Harmony

The verses are harmonised by a simple four-chord pattern (Bm G♯ G F♯).

The bridge consists of a set of chords, descending in semitones and then ascending again.

Master Blaster (Jammin') (1980)

A tribute to reggae in which he has captured the style of roots reggae (including a mention of Bob Marley in the fourth verse). Reggae features include the dominant bass line, the shuffle rhythm and drum pattern (especially the explosive fills), and the offbeat guitar chords. More specifically the roots feel has been achieved by the organ in the background and particularly the unaccompanied solos alternating with the bass during the instrumental middle section, suggesting the techniques of dub (see page 106).

Structure and harmony

Verse and chorus. Instrumental 'dub' middle section.

The harmony of the verse is a simple set of chords descending in parallel:

> Bm   A   G   F♯   E   Bm   A

BOB MARLEY

Marley is generally credited with having given reggae mass appeal, particularly through anthems like *No Woman No Cry*. Marley's brand of reggae was rooted in the Rastafarian faith, in which the plight of black people as the dispossessed children of Africa is expressed in Old Testament references.

Three Little Birds (1977)

Structure and harmony

Like many reggae songs this opens with the chorus and proceeds to the verse. Although the harmonies are confined to three primary triads the chorus derives its presence from the steady harmonic rhythm:

A	E	A	D	A	E	D	A

The overall structure is simple:

Chorus	Verse 1	Chorus	Verse 1 repeat	Chorus repeat to fade

Style and instrumentation

The reggae feel is established by the bass line (doubled by piano) with typical repeated notes on the first beat. The organ riff in the treble is based on a simple broken chord figuration – like a five-finger exercise – and this also serves as a memorable hook to the song. The reggae feel is completed by the offbeat guitar chords and the drum pattern with its syncopated snare drum rimshots.

One Love (1968)

This song achieved world fame because it was during the One Love Peace Concert in 1978 in Jamaica that Marley invited the leaders of his country's two political parties onto the stage to join hands as a sign of reconciliation in what had been a very violent election campaign. It is easy to tell from the lyrics that Marley's own position was religious rather than political.

Structure and harmony

Like most of Marley's songs this opens with the chorus. The verse is built round a three-chord pattern – VI IV I (Gm E♭ B♭) – and the move at the start of the verse into relative minor harmony has a settling effect after the more flamboyant choruses.

Melody

The chorus features a call-and-response effect between Marley and the backing vocalists. The melody and words are both extremely simple and lend themselves to participation by the audience.

The more lyrical verses contain the main message of the song and, with the choruses, give the impression, if not of gospel, then of a prayer meeting.

Redemption Song (1980)

Style and structure

This was performed and recorded as a folk song with voice and acoustic guitar. Like many folk songs, *Redemption Song* is essentially story-telling: the verses come first with the more reflective chorus later (unlike most other songs by Marley in which the chorus is stated first).

The single-line melody at the start sets the scene, and the folk feel is sustained by melodies which are based on five-note patterns around the notes of the harmony.

Harmony

The chorus derives its strength from the harmonic rhythm:

|D |G |C D |G |C D |Em |C D |G |C D |G |

In effect this is a set of cadences – one every two bars, including an interrupted one in bars 5 and 6 – and these have a sense of finality, like an 'amen'. This is enhanced by the echo-like repetition of the last two bars.

The ending is unresolved, the final harmony being V7c (D7/A). Doubtless this is deliberate, given the message of the lyrics, but it is a radical way to end a song.

MICHAEL JACKSON

Like Stevie Wonder, Jackson was a child prodigy. Apart from outselling almost every other songwriter he set new standards in production, combining synthesised backings with the orchestrations of his producer, the composer and arranger Quincy Jones.

Beat It (1982)

In *Beat It* Jackson developed a mix of soul, dance and heavy rock – a forerunner of contemporary R&B and techno.

Structure and harmony

Based on a two-bar riff over a pair of alternating chords (I and flat VII), the song alternates verse and chorus with a guitar solo in the middle.

The introduction, with its distorted and chorused guitar chords, has an element of mystery about it before the dance groove begins. It is repeated later in the song as an introduction to the guitar solo.

Instrumentation

The riff, which is heard in the introduction and the choruses, is played by the guitar, heavily overdriven so that it has a rock rather than a soul feel.

The drum part contains no fills or other decoration but sustains interest partly through its relentless energy but mainly because of a highly effective rhythmic device: every fourth bar (and sometimes every other bar) the second bass drum hit is delayed by a quaver, leaving a 'hole' in the backing:

Jackson maintains a relatively light backing in the verses: a quiet chordal backing from an electric piano and a subtle guitar riff. He reserves most of the complexity for the choruses, where he layers backing vocals (including percussive shouts).

The guitar solo in the middle is played by heavy metal virtuouso Eddie Van Halen.

Billie Jean (1983)

Structure

Jackson adopts a standard form based on the 12-bar blues, a structure which he also used in *The Way You Make Me Feel*.

Verse 1	12 bars
Verse 2	8 bars (omits the last four of the 12-bar structure)
Bridge	8 bars
Chorus	12 bars
Repeat (verse 3, verse 4, bridge, chorus)	
Repeat chorus to fade	

Harmony

The verses and chorus are based on the I, IV, V blues chords, but it is the eight-bar bridge that sets up the chorus, a change of harmony leading to the dominant:

| VI | I | VI | I | VI | I | IV | V |

Instrumentation

The electronic backing – the drum machine, synthesised bass line and synthesised strings – are obvious from the start, and provide a strong looped backing groove for the song.

Note the guitar in the last four bars of the choruses and the live strings entering in verse 4. These are progressively added to the arrangement, but the texture is always kept very sparse. Jackson alternates instrumental colours as well as combining them.

ELTON JOHN

Before achieving fame as a singer/songwriter, Elton John had a classical training and was an established and experienced session musician. He has sustained a songwriting career for over thirty years with an effortless succession of memorable hits.

Crocodile Rock (1972)

Style

A rock'n'roll pastiche with its 'low-tech' organ backing chords and wordless chorus performed by a backing singer with staccato guitar arpeggios. This passage is possibly intended to be a parody of '50s and '60s hits such as *Poetry in Motion* (Johnny Tillotson) and *Speedy Gonzales* (Pat Boone).

Harmony and Structure

The song is based on regular patterns of four chords, each lasting two bars, but despite the regular phrase structure interest is sustained by unexpected changes of harmony and chord pattern.

Intro	Based on the standard I VI IV V chord pattern (G Em C D)
Verses 1 and 2	A new four-chord pattern: G Bm C D
Chorus/middle	The fact that the lyrics are the same each time this passage is repeated suggests a chorus, although the change of harmony (to an E minor chord) creates the feeling of a bridge (with a chorus to follow). Indeed, these 16 bars lead to the wordless vocal section referred to above – which, because it opens on tonic harmony, sounds more like a true chorus. Such ambiguities are typical of John's songwriting.
	This passage introduces a further set of four-chord patterns: Em A7 D7 G and E A7 D7 C
	The final two chords lead to the next section, starting on a chord of G. We would normally expect these two chords, being V and IV, to be the other way round (i.e. finishing on the dominant harmony), but V–IV at the end of a section is a typical blues progression.
Chorus	A return to the chords of the introduction.

Philadelphia Freedom (1975)

Although this song was originally written as an anthem for the team of tennis champion Billie Jean King it was heavily influenced by the black R&B sound of 1970s Philadelphia, which featured strong soul-like backings combined with lush orchestral arrangements.

What characterises the song is its seamless melody lasting some 50 bars. It is sustained by a variety of devices: varied phrase lengths and harmonic rhythm, abrupt contrasts of harmony and passing modulations.

Style and instrumentation

Note the flute **arabesques** in the introduction and the disco-like regular crotchet beat in the drums. Woven round the vocal part for much of the song is a wonderful counter-melody for the violins, played with slinky portamento. Note also the horn fill leading to the chorus.

Structure

One of the features that sustains the melody is the way repeated passages are handled: they are fewer and shorter as the song goes on, such that the chorus, to which these sections lead, has no repeated phrases at all in its 16 bars:

A	A	B	B	C	D	E
Verse 1	**Verse 2**	**Bridge**.................................				**Chorus**
8 bars	8 bars	4 bars	4 bars	4 bars	4 bars	16 bars (8+8)

At the same time the harmonic rhythm accelerates. For example, in the opening eight-bar verses the first four bars have the same harmony, then the number of chords increases:

| B♭ | | | | | C7 | B♭m6/D♭ Cm7 | B♭ | F7sus4 |

This technique is extended in the other sections, particularly in the chorus, which opens with a chord (B♭7) lasting two bars, the harmonic rhythm then shifting to one chord per bar, then two, and finishing with five chords squeezed into a single bar in the final cadence.

Harmony

Verses   These are centred around tonic harmony (but note the use of chord II – Cm – as a substitute dominant).

Bridge   The harmony shifts to the subdominant, giving the passage a strong and typical bridge/middle section feel. It is not until the middle of this section – and, interestingly, at bar 25, exactly half way though the 50-bar verse/bridge/chorus structure – that there is an abrupt shift to a more remote A♭ chord. The chromatic progressions which make up the last eight bars of the bridge could lead to almost any related key for the chorus, and although this opens on the tonic chord of B♭ the inclusion of the seventh (also stated in the melody) lends a rather unstable feel.

Chorus   The 16-bar chorus might be described as a typical binary structure. The first half cadences with a modulation to the dominant, F. However, rather than returning to the tonic there is a further modulation to the relative G minor which begins the second half of the chorus. The chorus closes in the tonic.

Blue Eyes (1988)

One of the few songs by Elton John that incorporates a 32-bar structure, albeit heavily modified. The AABA is structured as follows:

Bars 1–8	First phrase opening in B♭ and ending on the dominant.
Bars 9–16	First phrase repeated with a second-time bar leading to D minor.
Bars 17–26	Opens with the feel of a standard middle-eight section in the relative minor, but does not follow the standard eight-bar pattern.
Bars 17–19	New and contrasting melody for three bars.
Bars 20–24	A repeat of bars 2–8 of the A Section compressed into five bars.
Bars 25–26	Two-bar turnaround for a *da capo* repeat.

Harmony

Note the descending bass line in bars 1–4 and the inversions it creates. Note also the E♭11 in bar 5. This chromatic subdominant chord lends the song a very bluesy feel (this is where a change to the subdominant would occur in a 12-bar blues).

Can You Feel the Love Tonight? (2002)

Although this is quite a simple song it shows how melody and harmony can be exploited to create contrast between verses and chorus. It also shows how Elton John adapts his songwriting style to the words of a different lyricist. Here the words are by Tim Rice, whose metre is more regular than in the lyrics of John's more usual collaborator, Bernie Taupin. As a consequence this song is more episodic in structure, to match the regular rhyming pattern of the lines (ABCB).

Harmony

For the most part this revolves around I, IV and V. Note how the verse opens on the subdominant, a two-chord pattern (E♭, B♭).

The composer avoids a strong sense of cadence by avoiding root positions for both tonic and dominant chords throughout the verse. Not until we get to the chorus do we hear a firm cadence with chords in root position.

Melody

The verses are characterised by melodic phrases based on stepwise movement, though with a leap at the end of some phrases. Note how ascending leaps are balanced by descending ones, and how the melodic movement becomes more disjunct as we build to the chorus. The chorus is contrasted, opening with a memorable and optimistic octave leap and characterised by arpeggio figurations.

CHAPTER 9

Islands and Continents

Almost all popular music is a mix of cultures, but some styles originating around the world have a special flavour of their own. In this chapter we will explore some of them: reggae from the West Indies, salsa from South America, bhangra from the Indian sub-continent and Celtic popular music from Ireland and Scotland.

Reggae

Reggae has a characteristic offbeat chordal accompaniment developed from the rock'n'roll piano playing styles of performers like Fats Domino and Jerry Lee Lewis:

There are many different styles of reggae. Ska is in a shuffle rhythm and usually in a major key. It has a characteristic bass drum stress on the third beat (known as a 'drop' pattern):

Rock Steady is closer to the simple four-in-a-bar patterns of rock'n'roll with a stress on the second and fourth beats:

In England during the 1980s, reggae was prominent in the charts with hits by Aswad, Eddie Grant and UB40. The Police and Madness also wrote many songs with a Carribean influence. However, reggae is usually associated with the island of Jamaica and the songs of artists like Jimmy Cliff, Burning Spear, Toots and the Maytals and Bob Marley (see page 97).

Their style is often called roots reggae because the lyrics are about the tribulations of black West Indians and their spiritual links with the African homeland. Many roots artists follow the Rastafarian faith, which draws parallels between the Israelites of the Old Testament and the African slaves.

Roots songs are often in a minor key with a prominent bass line, and the root of the chord is typically stressed with repeated notes. The drums stress the third beat, with the bass drum doubled by a rimshot on the snare (one end of the stick is pivoted against the inside rim so the stick touches the opposite side of the drum).

Many songs are based on a two-chord pattern, though most of Bob Marley's songs employ an extended chord sequence.

Another characteristic of roots reggae is the technique of **dub**. A dub version of a song would often be recorded after the release of the original, with the musicians returning to the studio to remix the song, adding effects and new parts. Typically, the mix concentrated on the drum and bass parts and wove new ideas around them, cutting and mixing to produce a new set of recorded tracks based on the original. Very often it would be an instrumental version, so the DJ or MC could add new lyrics, often rapped or **toasted** (rapped on a monotone in tune with the underlying chord).

A common technique was the use of a **delay line** which would allow the engineer to repeat a drum part or a snatch of melody by momentarily routing it through the delay unit and leaving it echoing in the mix. This is a forerunner of a technique employed by the modern DJ who uses a record deck to spin a drum pattern repeatedly to create a **breakbeat**. In many ways the technological achievements of the reggae artists of the '70s paved the way for contemporary club and urban music (see Chapter 10).

The instrumentation of a reggae band is the same as a rock one: lead, rhythm and bass guitars, keyboards (a retro Hammond organ sound is popular), drums and vocals. This can be augmented by flutes, a brass section and additional percussion, especially congas.

Composing a reggae backing

This is a lesson for groups of four. Learning to compose and play a reggae pattern is a good rhythmic training exercise; it is harder to play on the offbeats and master the syncopations than you might think.

Resources
Keyboards and/or guitars.
Drum and bass parts can also be played on a keyboard.

Task
Start by listening to some examples of reggae (*Three Little Birds* by Bob Marley would be a good choice).

Then choose a pair of chords for the keyboard or guitar (the example below uses Dm and C). Play on the offbeats, one chord per bar.

Now add the bass drum on the third beat to establish the drop pattern, and a syncopated backbeat for the snare in the second bar:

Now add the bass:

Finally, try adding a melodic phrase for keyboard.

To the teacher

All the students should be able to create a simple reggae backing with an offbeat pattern and a bass drum part. Most of them will be able to add a bass line and a syncopated backbeat.

Prior learning Some keyboard work. Understanding metre.

Extension Make sure each performer remembers his or her pattern. It will be used to learn about dub – see next page.

Adding variety – creating a dub

An example of dub occurs on two classic albums (now released together on a CD) by Burning Spear: *Marcus Garvey* and its dub version *Garvey's Ghost*. Here, each of the original tracks are remixed, and the rather mechanical effect of the engineer fading instruments in and out of the mix gives the changes of texture a unique quality, completely different to the way the music would have sounded if the players had started and stopped in a live performance. The techniques represent the birth of electronic popular music.

A dub can also be played live. Here the instruments drop out dramatically, usually leaving the bass playing solo. Then they re-enter one by one in different combinations – a textural device which was the forerunner of the **breakdown** section in contemporary club music (see Chapter 10).

EXERCISE ♫ and ♫♪

Creating a dub passage is good practice in texture management. It can be done live (as an extension to the lesson above) or on a computer.

The two-bar patterns should all start off together. You will need to plan the structure of the dub: who is playing where, and for how long?

It will help if you arrange the dub using a diagram similar to the track display on a computer. If you are using a computer you just need to copy the two-bar segments to the positions you want by dragging with the mouse (alternatively you can copy everything across and then erase the bits you don't want).

Guitar					▓	▓	▓	▓	▓	▓	▓	▓				
Keyboard									▓	▓	▓	▓	▓	▓	▓	▓
Snare drum														▓	▓	▓	▓
Bass drum														▓	▓	▓	▓
Bass	▓	▓	▓	▓	▓	▓	▓	▓				▓	▓	▓	▓	▓

Salsa

Salsa originated in Cuba but, along with the term **Latino**, has become a general term for popular music with a Latin American influence. It includes dance music based on the Cuban **rhumba**, as well as music with a Brazilian **samba** influence. Chapter 11 includes a whole class exercise in samba playing, and might serve as a preparation for the study of salsa.

The driving rhythms of Latin America have always been popular with songwriters. An early example was the chart hit *La Bamba* by Ritchie Valens. During the '60s Carlos Santana perfected his own style of Latin rock, a stylistic influence obvious on the album *Abraxas*. During the '80s and '90s Latino came to prominence in the work of Gloria Estefan and Ricky Martin, whose *Livin' la Vida Loca* was a major chart hit.

Salsa is characterised primarily by its rhythm. Latin rhythm usually consists of several one- or two-bar patterns, each played by a different instrument and based around a fundamental rhythm called *clave* (see also page 10) which is usually played by the claves; hence its name. Woven around this part is a rhythmic counterpoint involving three basic types of percussion: shakers (e.g. maracas, chocolo, cabasa, eggs), instruments with a sharp attack (e.g. claves, cowbells, woodblocks) and drums (e.g. congas, bongos, timbales). Below is a typical grouping broken down into parts. The tempo of salsa is fast – not less than 120 BPM.

The shakers maintain a continuous semiquaver pattern:

Then we add the *clave* (the same rhythm as on page 10, but with note-values halved):

Additional woodblocks and bells can play syncopated and accented patterns around the clave. (There are more ideas for rhythms on page 129.)

Congas are added for depth:

The kit drum part tends to be quite simple:

In addition to the percussion, salsa features other instruments – a brass section consisting mainly of trumpets is very popular. Some of the solos can go stratospherically high (as on Ricky Martin's *The Cup of Life* – the official song of the 1998 World Cup). When used as an ensemble the instruments tend to play mainly in unison, adding short, syncopated riffs. In *Conga* (Gloria Estefan) the trumpets alternate with the singer, setting up a furious dialogue.

The example below is a typically fragmented phrase for unison brass which really needs to be understood as part of the backing texture rather than as a flowing melody. The effect of several trumpets playing these syncopated phrases in unison is very powerful:

Another characteristic feature of Latino instrumentation is the use of a piano to fill in the backing with a broken chord pattern, typically played in octaves or fifteenths (a tricky technique for the beginner – you may have to try it with two players). This is a common textural device and can be heard in both the songs mentioned above.

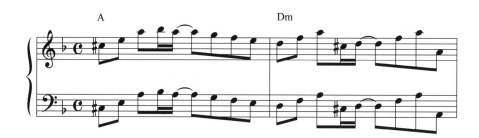

The harmony is rarely complicated, and, because of its origins in *flamenco*, the key is frequently a minor one. Whole verses are often based on a single chord, or pair of chords (as in the two examples above, which alternate tonic and dominant). The bass line might be a driving riff with broken chord figuration, sometimes played in 'slap style' (see page 57).

Longer chord progressions can consist of parallel movement with a flamenco guitar feel:

EXERCISES ♩♪ and ♪♪♪

Equipment
Keyboards, hand-held percussion.

Tasks
Compose and perform a set of one-bar percussion patterns based on the examples above, to go with this bass line:

Now add a syncopated broken chord pattern for piano, played in octaves if you can.

Now add a trumpet melody or a vocal part based on these simple Latin American words:

La, la fiesta,
La, la, musica

The chorus of Ricky Martin's *The Cup of Life* has a great football chant chorus: 'Go, go, go, olé, olé, olé!'

STUDY PROJECTS ♩♪

Latin American popular music covers a wealth of styles. Using the internet, find out about some of them: the tango (from Argentina), the bossa nova (a slower and gentler style), and also the different types of samba pattern (including the meringue and the batucada).

Many of these styles will be among the preset patterns available on a drum machine. Listen and compare them. How do they differ? Try them at different tempi. Do they use the same percussion instruments?

Bhangra

The term *bhangra* has come to mean 'Indian pop music'; but more strictly speaking it is a Punjabi celebratory dance, traditionally performed during the April Bhaisakhi festival to the accompaniment of a bass drum (the *dhol*) and a singer.

Interest in South Asian music has grown tremendously in the last few years, although both the Beatles and the Rolling Stones featured a sitar in their songs during the mid-'60s (the Beatles on *Norwegian Wood* and *Within You Without You*, and the Rolling Stones on *Paint it Black*).

Contemporary bhangra embraces a wide range of styles, and uses traditional instruments alongside synthesisers and samplers. It is sung in English as well as the authentic Punjabi, and it has absorbed the styles of urban club and hip-hop, as well as the extravagant 'Bollywood' Indian film music style. Traditional instruments are sometimes sampled and then looped into the mix on a computer (see page 119). There is a very good guide to Indian instruments on the website www.indianmusicals.com

The most common percussion instruments are:

tabla	a pair of drums (bass and treble)
dholak	a double-ended tenor drum
dhol	a powerful bass drum associated with traditional bhangra

Usually the dhol provides a bass part with tabla or dholak adding a decorative part above. Many artists use electronic tablas which take the form either of a sound module, to be played with MIDI drum pads (see page 67), or a synthesiser with keys. Here is a typical pattern – it has a feel similar to a 'jazz quaver': the quavers are shorter than triplet quavers but not as short as the semiquavers in a ♪. ♪ pattern.

The rhythmic pattern consists of a typical subdivision of the bar into 2 + 3 + 3. Indian classical music is built on cycles of subdivided beats known as *talas*.

Of all the Indian string instruments the *sitar* is perhaps the best known (though little used in bhangra). Also common is the simpler four-string *tampura*, used to provide a drone and also available in electronic form as a sound module. The *sarangi* and *tumbi* are bowed, and are popular with well-known artists like Rishi Rich and Panjabi MC.

The Indian harmonium is a keyboard instrument with hand-operated bellows. It is often replaced on recordings by a synthesiser because the mechanical action can be quite intrusive on a microphone (the general MIDI accordion sound is quite close). However, it is important to try to reproduce the effect of its one-handed technique of playing: one hand plays while the other operates the bellows. Synthesised strings are often employed for Bollywood-type songs.

The harmony of bhangra tends to be simple – one or two chords, sometimes repeated in two-bar blocks (see below). Traditional instruments often retain their original tunings (the systems of South Asian tunings would fill another book) but arrangements tend to adopt Westernised minor modes. One of these is the mode obtained by playing a minor scale starting on its dominant. A popular key is B♭ minor (with flat seventh), because on a harmonium this can be played quite easily as two four-note groups, with the thumb playing the white notes and fingers 1–3 the black ones (the little finger is not used):

However, because this is not an easy key for some instruments and beginners, it is also shown below in A minor, starting on E:

Here is a typical melody:

Rishi Rich is one of the best-known bhangra artists and is in demand as a producer (including work on Britney Spears' *In the Zone*). His *Dance with You* is a typical mix of traditional and new: a two-bar rock drum pattern played on the dholak and a reggae-like pair of chords led by the sarangi.

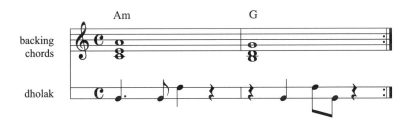

Panjabi MC also favours traditional instruments. His best known song is *Mundian To Bach Ke*, of which there is an equally well-known remix featuring the rapper Jay Z, called *Beware of the Boys*. The arrangement features a *tumbi* – a one-string fiddle normally employed to play the drone in a piece of sacred music, but here the player provides a plucked three-note riff which dominates the song. This is combined with a bass line sampled from the title theme of the *Nightrider* television series (a popular bass line with dance-music songwriters) to produce a rich arrangement despite its economical resources.

One of the first Indian artists to have achieved chart success is Apache Indian, whose song titles, like *Arranged Marriage* and *Drink Problems*, touch on social issues important to young Asian people. Coming from the cultural mix of England's West Midlands, his music shows the influence of reggae as well as bhangra. His vocal style is heavily West Indian: chanting (or **toasting**) over reggae-like offbeat chords – but with a tabla backing. Here is an example of toasting, with the characteristic lift at the end of the first phrase:

Me   friends all round gon-na   sing all the while. I'm   gon-na go sing-ing in the   rag-ga-muf-fin style.

Given the scale of the Bollywood film industry and its emphasis on music and dance, it is hardly surprising that its influence should be felt in popular songwriting. Bollywood films are notable for their production numbers – sometimes filmed in a single long take, and transported out of the context of the story to a fanciful and exotic location like the Swiss Alps. The film *Dil Se* includes the entire chorus dancing on the roof of a train as it snakes through the hills, filmed from a helicopter.

The successful Bollywood composer A R Rahman wrote the songs for the stage musical *Bombay Dreams*. It is very westernised, but provides a good illustration of the way South Asian music can be adapted to European instruments and audiences. Many of the songs are based on the minor mode illustrated above, and the opening sequence, *Bombay Awakes*, features an oboe (imitating the Indian *shehnai*) underscored by rich string chords. *Salaam Bombay*, an ensemble piece, is accompanied by a repeated note on the sitar (although it sounds synthesised on the recording). There is a two-bar rhythm with different subdivisions of the bar (3 + 3 + 2 followed by 3 + 2 + 3):

EXERCISES ♪♪ and ♪♪♪

Working in groups, devise a verse for a bhangra song in three parts: percussion, backing instrument and solo instrument.

For the percussion, choose a drum with a penetrating sound. Devise a subdivision of a 4/4 bar, then add a second bar with a different subdivision. Don't forget to swing the quavers.

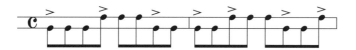

To complete the percussion, add a bass drum part (a dhol would be ideal but a passable sound can be obtained by damping a bass or tenor drum with one hand and striking it with a felt-headed timpani stick). The dhol often plays the outline rhythm of the tala.

Now choose a plucked-instrument sound on a keyboard and add a four-bar backing riff: three bars the same and the last one different (an A A A B pattern adopted by Panjabi MC).

Then add a solo. Choose a harmonium, organ or strings sound, using the notes of the minor mode illustrated above.

To the teacher

There is a performance project for the whole class based on *tala* on page 132.

Celtic popular music

Folk – or, to give it a more modern term, **traditional music** – has played a key role in the development of popular music, and has sometimes enjoyed commercial success as a style in its own right. In the '60s the music of Bob Dylan and Joan Baez – strophic songs with guitar accompaniment and a direct political message – spoke for a generation. On Dylan's album *Highway 61 Revisited* (1965) folk could be said to have 'gone electric', and this spawned a decade of folk-rock bands including, in England, Fairport Convention and Steeleye Span. The Dubliners have enjoyed four decades of success, teaming up with the Pogues for a chart hit in 1987 with *The Irish Rover*.

The concept of Celtic rock probably began with the Scottish band Big Country, whose 'bagpipe sound' was the result of two lead guitars playing heterophonically (see below), like an ensemble of bagpipes. The influence of traditional music and its instrumental and vocal techniques has been felt in the work of many subsequent bands: the vocal style of Dolores O'Riordan of the Cranberries is influenced by the tradition of Irish unaccompanied solo singing called *sean-nos*, and Sinead O'Connor has recorded a CD of traditional songs called *Sean-Nos Nua*.

The language of traditional music

Most traditional music is modal, the most common three modes being Mixolydian (a scale consisting of all the white notes on a piano from G to G), Dorian (the white notes from D to D) and Aeolian (the white notes from A to A).

The underlying harmonies typically include the major chord on the flat leading note (the 7th note of the mode) acting as a dominant and creating the characteristic modal feel at cadences. The submediant and, in a minor mode, the mediant (the chord of the 'relative major') are also common, as well as the usual tonic and subdominant.

Chords are often played with the 3rd missing – also a feature of vocal harmonisations – which gives the harmony a bare, drone-like feel. However, it is quite common for the instruments to play **heterophonically** – each playing its own version of the melody, either in unison or at the octave, without chordal support. The melody tends to be decorated with ornaments: upward and downward **grace notes**, **rolls** (known to classical instrumentalists as **turns**), and **slides**.

Although traditional instruments are acoustic, artists venturing into the popular field tend to mix these with amplified instruments. Some bands are entirely amplified – the Scottish band Runrig uses a rock guitar line-up, even when performing traditional songs. Their version of *Loch Lomond* is a show-stopping feature of their live act. The Irish band Clannad (which included Enya before she went solo) uses keyboards and, on some numbers, a drum kit. Their recorded vocals tend to use a lot of reverberation (see page 74), giving the sound a rather ethereal, dreamy quality.

Common acoustic instruments are the guitar, harp, fiddle (played without vibrato), flute (the Irish flute is made of wood and has a larger bore than the orchestral version), the tin whistle and the pipes – bagpipes in Scotland and Uillean pipes in Ireland. Percussion is simple: in Ireland the backing is provided by the *bodhran* (pronounced 'boron'), a hand-held tambour played with a double-ended beater. It has a slackly-tuned skin, to produce a 'thud' rather than a ringing drum tone.

Ideas for listening

The Chieftains have enjoyed enduring success as a traditional band, and are now so distinguished in their field they have joined that exclusive group of performers with whom everyone wants to work. They play traditional instruments, but have collaborated with a wide range of artists, some quite unexpected. Many of these collaborations are included on their CD *The Wide World Over*. Highlights are the magical *Redemption Song* by Bob Marley, performed by his son Ziggy alongside the Chieftains' Uillean pipes and flute; *The Rocky Road to Dublin* with the Rolling Stones, the latter's country-rock and blues guitar style marrying perfectly with the Irish ballad; and Sting singing in Gaelic on *Mo Ghile Mear*.

Clannad's performances of traditional songs tend to be conventional, lightly accompanied by guitars or harp, as in *Down by the Sally Gardens*. However, the band (and Enya's subsequent solo work) is perhaps better known for rich synthesised backings and vocal arrangements. The keyboards produce a blend of rich flute and choral sounds with strings, and are characterised by the spacings of the notes: not a 'two-handed' keyboard part, but fully orchestrated with a deep bass part and thick doublings (the opening string chords in Vaughan Williams' *Fantasia on a Theme by Thomas Tallis* will provide a guide to the number and spacing of the parts). The vocal parts are in **close harmony**, but often thickened electronically. In addition, reverberation is added to provide a rather mystical, church-like atmosphere. Solo instrumental work is provided by wind instruments, especially flute, and these, too, are 'distanced' in the mix by reverberation and delay.

I Will Find You, written for the 1992 film *The Last of the Mohicans* is a typically atmospheric composition. Although modal in feel, its chord progression (a repeating three-chord pattern) has a distinct 'pop' feel, supported by a rather ritualistic bass drum part and quiet ostinati:

| Cmaj7 | D | Em | | |

Composers and performers have been quick to spot the commercial potential of Irish music and dance, and it came to worldwide prominence in *Riverdance*. The show is a mix of styles, including Spanish flamenco, but the core performances are the traditional dance routines. The award-winning score, by Bill Whelan, adapts many of the traditional conventions for the theatre: for example the bohdran is replaced by a battery of tom-toms, slack-headed and played with sticks to produce an almost overpowering backing. Combined with the percussive effect of the dancers' tap shoes, there is a stamping drive that suggests African drumming.

On top of this backing, the melody instruments – fiddles are reserved for most of the fast numbers and flute for the slower ones – weave a series of jigs and reels. Drama is added through a number of devices. One possibility is to transpose the phrase up to a new harmony (a technique which is also used by film composers):

Usually it is transposed up a fourth, but in some numbers it moves progressively up by semitones.

One can also add rhythmic variety, subdividing the compound time signatures and introducing heavily syncopated patterns:

PERFORMANCE PROJECT ♪♪ and ♪♪♪

The tune below, by the author, is a hornpipe, with the quavers to be swung like jazz quavers. Its structure follows the conventional pattern of a traditional melody, consisting of an A section and a B section. It is in the Dorian mode, transposed to tonic A.

Try memorising the tune, as a traditional musician would do – A first, then B.

Make an arrangement for several instruments playing in unison or at the octave.

Start to put the ensemble together at a slower tempo. Some of the players might try experimenting with ornaments.

Now add a bohdran part. It may be easier to play this on a large tom-tom with sticks. The basic rhythm is:

Don't forget to swing the quavers.

Lastly, speed up to the standard hornpipe tempo of 132 BPM.

Follow up

Try a rock arrangement by adding a drum kit. Then add a bass line and chordal backing.

Use the internet to look up the difference between a jig, a reel and a hornpipe.

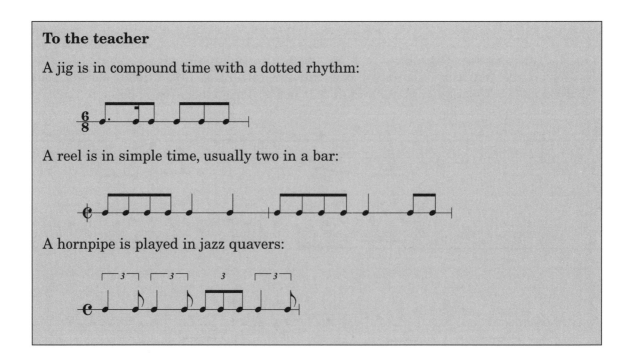

To the teacher

A jig is in compound time with a dotted rhythm:

A reel is in simple time, usually two in a bar:

A hornpipe is played in jazz quavers:

CHAPTER 10

Club and Urban

To the teacher

This chapter covers the styles of club dance and urban popular music, including hip hop, rap and R&B. There is a great diversity of styles, with many sub-genres, but it is not the purpose here to turn the teacher into a DJ or to keep pace with club culture. The aim is to explore what is possible in a school classroom.

The best way to learn about the styles is usually from the students themselves. Encourage them to bring in favourite recordings and discuss them. Also, record stores are worth a visit. The dance section will be divided into various sub-groupings, each with its own selection of CDs, and amongst these it is usually possible to find a budget compilation which contains typical examples and recent hits.

Some styles work better in the classroom than others. Generally those that feature sophisticated production techniques and vocals – like **trance**, **trip hop** and **garage** – tend to be harder to bring off (although there are some projects based on urban R&B below). The instrumental genres are the easiest. **Drum'n'bass** is an eclectic style whose fast, complex drum patterns offer many opportunities for creative rhythm work (listen to work by Roni Size). **Ambient**, the music played in the 'chill out' room, is slow and dreamy, with drifting chordal textures and hypnotic percussion (listen to Aphex Twin, or *Chill Out* by the KLF). Much **techno** is based on rock guitar samples (there are projects related to techno below, drawing on the work of one of the best known acts, the Chemical Brothers).

See also Fatboy Slim (page 53), the Prodigy (page 143) and the Streets (page 27).

LISTENING ♪

For many pop historians, contemporary dance music began with Donna Summer's *I Feel Love*. Although it was recorded in 1977, before MIDI and computers, it has lost none of its immediacy.

Donna Summer has been called the queen of disco. Although she was capable of vocal gymnastics, the vocals on *I Feel Love* are actually very simple, consisting of repeated phrases and vocalised passages. Much of the track is instrumental, and it is the treatment of instruments which marks the song out:

➤ electronic backing instruments and long instrumental interludes

➤ the backing pattern – a heavily syncopated one-bar loop which is transposed up and down in line with the chord sequence, establishing a powerful groove

> ➤ the drum pattern – an insistent bass drum in steady crotchet beats, now a trademark of much club dance music

> ➤ the breakdown section: at the end of the recording the texture thins out to the drum and bass and is then built up again, track by track. This, too, has become a characteristic feature of contemporary club music; it originates in dub reggae (see page 106)

Questions

How does the producer achieve variety?

In what order do the instruments appear during the breakdown?

The techniques of club music

Club music is computer-based, and might be described as the art of cut-and-paste. Its progress has gone hand in hand with the development of technology, particularly the sampler (see next page). Compositions are usually compiled on screen, and beginners may find it helpful to try one of the entry-level programs, like Dance eJay, Music Maker or GarageBand. These consist of an arrangement window into which you can drag pre-recorded samples using the mouse. The samples are all standard lengths – either one, two or four bars long – and can be copied very easily. They are all at the same tempo and in the same key, so they all fit together. It is easy to dismiss these programs as computer games, but you do have to think about structure. Despite the fact that club music is a repetitive style, it contains a great deal of subtlety. You also have to think about texture: a common mistake is to have too much going on at once. It might help to draw a map of the composition showing the tracks and the order of the verses, choruses and breakdowns.

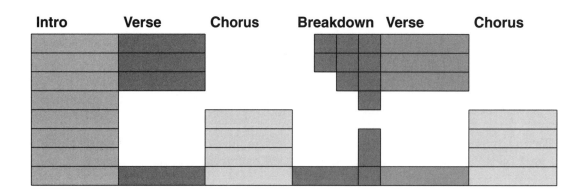

| Intro | Verse | Chorus | Breakdown | Verse | Chorus |

Sampling

Most of the tracks on a club song are compiled using sampled material. Hardware samplers were originally the norm, but most work is now done on computers using digital editing programs like Audition, Sound Forge, WaveLab and Pro Tools. Samples can come from one of three sources: CD, the internet (by downloading), or specially recorded.

Dozens of internet sites offer downloads, and samples CDs are obtainable by mail order and in specialist music stores, as advertised in the music technology journals and popular music press. There are CDs for every imaginable style, and each offers a comprehensive library of samples ranging from single percussion sounds to entire instrumental and vocal phrases. The samples are usually in two formats, one CD with **.wav** files (which, if you remember from Chapter 5, can only be heard if you load them into a music programme) and the other with audio (so you can play them). The tempo (in beats per minute – BPM) is usually identified; it is important to know the BPM because you may want to play two or more samples, and they have to be matched – see below.

Samples load onto the computer like any other file. Locate an audio track, place your CD (the one with the .wav files on) in the drive, go to **File** and click on **Import audio file**. When the **Open** box appears, go through the folders until you locate the sample you want to load. It will then appear as a short snippet on the selected track, which you can copy and paste. Don't forget that at this stage the program will only remember where the sample goes – not the sample itself. If you want to reload the song without the CD you will have to save the sample onto the computer's own hard drive.

You may wish to combine the sample with a MIDI track, so it is important to match the tempo of the track with the tempo of the sample. To do this put the program in **loop** mode. Now set the start of the loop point (the left hand locator) at the start of the sample, and the end of the loop point (the right hand locator) at the end of the nearest bar. The loop will contain both the sample and the gap at the end. Now start to change the tempo setting of the track. As you increase/decrease the tempo you will see the sample either shrink or stretch so it fits the loop. Let your ears be the judge. When the sample loops without a gap the tempo is correctly matched.

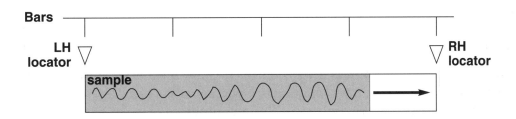

You may wish to combine the sample with other samples which are not at the same BPM. In this case you will have to stretch the sample itself. This is explained on pages 121–122.

More information about computer music can be found in Chapters 1, 5 and 6.

Recording your own samples

Samples can be made from other recordings or by recording live sounds. Background sounds and effects can be recorded first (for instance on MiniDisc), and then sampled, or samples can be made from commercial CDs – but remember that copyright exists in commercial recordings, so permission must be sought from the copyright holder.

Open your digital editing programme and connect the sound source (a CD player, microphone or keyboard) to the input of the computer sound card. It is advisable at this stage to check that the input level is not distorted. (This might be done by opening the master volume control, on the control panel, and listening. You may have to switch the volume control from playback to record.)

Now click on the record button. You may see a box asking you to select features of the recording, for instance:

Stereo or mono	Stereo is preferable, but bear in mind that this will take up two audio tracks, doubling the amount of memory needed.
Sample rate	This is the number of digital 'photographs' per second. The computer usually defaults at 44,100. Treble sounds, like strings and cymbals, will require this many samples for accuracy, but if you are sampling a bass instrument and want to save some memory you can choose a slower rate. This may also help the computer – an old model with a slow processor is liable to crash if too many complex samples are played at once.
8 or 16 bit	This refers to the computer code that the sample will be coded into. 16-bit is more accurate than 8-bit but, again, it will require more processing, so for a simple sound like a drum you may manage with 8-bit.

Now press 'Record' and play the instrument or the section of the CD that contains the sample. You don't need to be precise, as you can trim the sample to its exact size later. When you stop recording you should see the recording displayed as a waveform on the computer. Check that it is a satisfactory recording and, if it is, save it now so you don't lose it.

Trimming

If you have recorded too much (it is always better to allow a wide margin), you can trim the sample to size. Use the mouse to highlight a portion of the sample (in the same way as you would highlight a portion of text). Put the program into loop mode, and start playback.

Now look at the diagram at the top of the next page. Using the mouse, move the start and end points until the loop contains all the material you want. Then make fine adjustments to the start and end points with the mouse until the sample is contained within the loop and repeats smoothly.

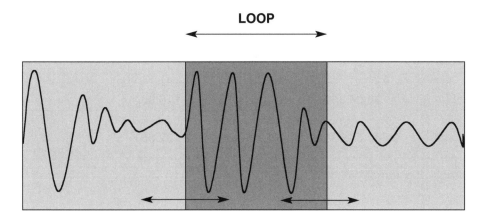

LOOP

For a drum loop or riff, you will need to make sure that the sample loops continuously without a hiccup in the beat. When you are satisfied, open the **Edit** menu and select **Trim**. The portions you don't want will be deleted (if you make a mistake click on **Undo**). Then save the newly trimmed sample.

Adding effects

Samples can be processed in various ways. One is to **normalise**. This maximises the sound and gives you the best possible result. There is also a range of effects like those on a mixing desk: reverb, echo and so on. If you intend to add effects, it is better to save the results as separate samples, rather than irreversibly change the one you started with.

Time stretching

If you want to combine samples which have a different BPM or are in different keys, you will have to match them.

Most digital editing programmes have a time-stretch function which allows you to change the BPM of a sample, transpose it or stretch it so that it fits another one. The function usually takes the form of a calculator showing the length and BPM of the original. The length of the sample is usually expressed as follows:

00   : 00   : 00   . 000
hours   : minutes : seconds . fractions of seconds

You can use the mouse to click on the values and change them; the calculator is interactive – that is, the other values will change to show the final length, the final BPM and the percentage change (i.e. by how much you have stretched or reduced the original). Remember the rule:

Making the sample *shorter* will make it play *faster*.
Making the sample *longer* will make it play *slower*.

The example on the next page shows a sample which is 4.388 seconds long and 120 BPM. The next line shows how much you would have to shorten it by to change its BPM to 137. Note that the final BPM is actually 137.331; the figures may not always work out exactly, and you may have to make fine adjustments to get as close as you can to 137.

The percentage figure shows that we have shrunk the sample to 87.38% of its original length – that is, we have made it shorter to achieve a faster BPM.

Original length 00:00:04.388	**Original tempo** 120.00
Final length 00:00:03.834	**Final tempo** 137.331
Percentage of original 87.38%	

If you want to try it out, click OK and have a listen. On most programs it is possible to undo if you are not satisfied.

Be warned: matching samples takes a lot of patience. Depending on the accuracy of the software, it can be rather hit and miss, and there is a limit to how far you can stretch a sample before it starts to sound distorted.

Some programs offer a technique for stretching drum samples and percussion called **beat slicing**. Here, the computer leaves the sounds themselves and stretches only the gaps in between, leaving a less distorted result.

Planning the composition

The process of composing club music is unique in music. It is more like making a film: first you compile all your recorded material, then go into the editing room to fit it all together. The club composer samples all the material needed (and records any extra MIDI parts), then turns it into a composition.

The final version is prepared in much the same way as a recording is mastered. Effects are added and a stereo mix made (see page 74). One feature of club music is **autopan**, whereby the sound moves automatically from the speakers on one side to those on the other, a spectacular effect on a large club PA system.

Not all club music is prerecorded. A DJ will often improvise with a combination of samples and record decks. In their simplest form, DJ decks consist of two turntables connected to a mixer, so it is possible to switch from one to the other. Two crucial features are the **slip mat**, which allows the DJ to hold a record steady while the turntable spins beneath it, and a **speed control** that enables the tempi of two records to be matched exactly, one following another without a break. DJs now have a battery of equipment, including CD decks and computers, so that samples can be added to the mix as well as raps and voice-overs.

PROJECTS

To the teacher

The following songs are all well known and cover a range of styles. They can serve as listening material or as models for composition projects.

First, a word of caution. These styles of music often come with a 'parental advisory' sticker on the CD cover. Young people listen to this music outside school for much of the time, and attitudes vary and change over time. When the Rolling Stones recorded *Let's Spend the Night Together* in 1967 it caused uproar in some parts of the press; now it is regularly played on Radio 2 and one of its composers has a knighthood. Notwithstanding contradictions like this, it is up to the individual teacher to decide, in the end, where to draw the line in the classroom.

The lyrics of rap are sometimes controversial, but many of them are extremely witty. Public Enemy, for example, recorded chat shows in which listeners had telephoned in to complain about the group and its material, and then sampled the complaints for inclusion in their songs (for example in the opening track on *Fear of a Black Planet*). Many rap crews have a cult following, but Eminem has achieved wide recognition (see also page 126 for a commentary on his song *Stan*) for his deft way with language. This can be quite explicit, so teachers are advised to review any track before playing it to the class.

Basement Jaxx

Basement Jaxx is a London-based act with a succession of **house** hits in the UK charts, many of which have become summer dance-floor anthems on the Ibiza club scene. House is a more commercial style of dance music, less aggressive than techno, and often draws on the energy of Latin American rhythms.

Rendez-vu is constructed entirely on a repeated one-bar guitar sample: two chords per bar, with a slight flamenco feel (Spanish and Latin American influences are popular with club acts working in the Balearic Islands).

Points to note:

➤ the drum pattern – typical house style with an insistent crotchet beat on the bass drum and a quaver offbeat (here provided by a shaker)

➤ the vocals – a mixture of nonsense 'scat' and simple lyrics heavily **vocoded**, an effect which artificially harmonises the voice and modulates the added part

➤ sustained string chords in the background

➤ a breakdown section featuring a guitar solo – note how the verse is re-established with a variant of the original guitar sample

PROJECT ♪♪ and ♪♪♪

Devise a two-chord pattern (see page 31 in the chapter on harmony).

Record this on the computer – either using MIDI or making your own sample by recording a guitar or keyboard.

Use this as the basis for a composition, repeating it and building layers on top like Basement Jaxx. Start with the bass drum, adding other percussion and a part for synthesiser.

Extension

Devise a wordless vocal part.

Devise a central breakdown section with an instrumental solo.

Samba Magic is characterised by its backing of Latin percussion. The harmonies are not as simple as in *Rendez-vu* but are a succession of two- and four-chord patterns.

Points to note:

➤ The percussion – mainly Latin American drums and shakers, the underlying drum sounds being drawn from the so-called '808 kit', referring to the sounds of the Roland 808 drum machine which was popular with early dance composers (the electronic handclap can be heard clearly). Note the background detail in the percussion, and the subtle changes as the song progresses.

➤ The vocals are very sparse (a few sampled phrases), the melodic interest being concentrated in the quite jazzy solos, played on a synthesiser – there is a good one in the breakdown, with handclap accompaniment.

PROJECT ♪♪ and ♪♪♪

Devise a set of one-bar percussion patterns based on Latin American rhythms (see page 107).

Add a bass drum and cymbal, and compose an introduction in which the percussion enters one by one, building to a full texture.

Now devise a two- or four-chord pattern (see page 34) for synthesiser – you may find that a rhythmic part for piano will work best, rather than something softer-edged like strings.

Use these elements as a backing track to support a series of instrumental solos.

Techno

Techno is characterised by its rock guitar samples and drum patterns. It often features simple, chanted vocals – perhaps a repeated phrase (such as 'The brothers gonna work it out' in the example by the Chemical Brothers, below).

Leave Home (the Chemical Brothers) includes a typical techno breakdown during which the percussion gradually builds in intensity, mainly by shortening the note values from crotchets through quavers and semiquavers to a complex repeated fill pattern.

Body Rock (Moby) also includes a breakdown in which the parts are thinned out to a bare texture and then built up again, climaxing in a re-entry of the verse. Note the processed vocal part, distanced in the mix with an exaggerated mid-range tone so it sounds like a tinny telephone voice (see page 74 for how to do this using the **equaliser** effect).

PROJECT ♪♪♪ and ♪♪♪♪

The commercial music world is often thought to involve a cultural split between guitar-based rock and computerised music. Techno is an opportunity to bridge that gap.

Create a drum track either using a sample library or by composing a MIDI pattern.

Working with a guitarist, record a selection of riffs and strummed patterns, using your drum track as a guide. Make a set of guitar samples using this recorded material. It will be easier if you record the drums first, but if you want to be adventurous you can record the guitar first and then time-stretch a drum sample to fit.

Compile a techno composition using your drum and guitar samples.

Extension

Devise and record a simple chanted vocal part.

Devise a breakdown in which the drums progressively accelerate through the note values:

Eminem

The Real Slim Shady has the feel of music hall about it: a two-bar backing pattern featuring a comic harpsichord riff (a parody of silent film mystery music) and a rapping crew who establish a quick-fire dialogue with Eminem. The backing serves as a vehicle for the rappers and is unvaried throughout, only the final verse being decorated by a countermelody.

Stan is a very dark tale and uses a sample from Dido's *Thank You*. Only late in the performance do we realise that Dido's song is being played on a car radio as Stan deliberately crashes the car (although the opening, with its crackly sample, provides a clue). The focus of the rap is a letter from a fan to his idol, the final verse being the idol's letter of reply. *Stan* is really a short radio play, full of black humour.

> ## PROJECTS ♪ and ♪♪
>
> 1   Devise a rap for more than one performer to tell a story about a comic event. The narrative should be divided between the rappers.
>
> 2   Devise a story to tell over a backing beat. Include sampled sound effects to provide background.

R&B

Although it usually depends on a strong singer to sell the song, contemporary R&B is often based on a very simple backing.

Brother (Ms Dynamite) has a simple one-bar electronic drum pattern and an acoustic guitar playing an arpeggio accompaniment. The choruses are enhanced by backing vocals (but these are confined to a **homophonic** texture in support of the lead singer) and by the addition of a little **delay** (see page 75) in the middle section.

Piano and I (Alicia Keys) is based on Beethoven's 'Moonlight' Sonata (Op. 27 No. 2), a performance of which forms the basic track around which the others are layered: close harmony backing vocals and sample drums. Alicia Keys speaks the lyrics. In the second half of the song, only the first bar of the Beethoven is used, and this is looped to the end of the song.

PROJECTS ♪♪♪ and ♪♪♪♪

1 Devise a backing track using a drum sample, then add a track for acoustic guitar or keyboard. It will be easier if you start with the drums and use that as a guide for the other instrument.

Choose a four-chord pattern (see page 34) and devise an arpeggio backing figuration.

2 Choose a classical piano piece as the basis for a composition. (Alicia Keys was herself classically trained. You might need to work with a pianist on this.) Possible suitable pieces are:

Bach: Prelude in C (No. 1 from the *Forty Eight Preludes and Fugues*)
Beethoven: *Sonata Pathetique*, slow movement (No. 8, Op. 13)
Schubert: Impromptu in G♭ major, Op. 90
Chopin: one of the Nocturnes or Preludes

As in the projects above, it may be easier if you select a suitable drum pattern and record it first, to act as a guide for recording the piano track.

When you have combined the piano and drums, try adding a countermelody for a solo voice (wordless) or a melody instrument. If you are feeling adventurous you could try adding backing chords for vocals or perhaps strings, but you will have to work out the underlying chords of the classical piece you have chosen.

Alicia Keys is not the only artist to have adapted classical music as the basis for a composition. Listen to some of the CDs by Café Del Mar: orchestral and operatic works with a gentle ambient backing.

CHAPTER 11

Performing Projects for the Class

Samba

Samba is the percussion music of the Brazilian carnival and is played by a marching band as the players and dancers follow the carnival procession. Although it is ideally played by authentic instruments these can be substituted with a little ingenuity for a performance project that will occupy the whole class and provide experience of playing syncopated rhythms.

The instruments of samba are as follows:

Repinique A tenor-sized drum played with sticks by the leader (who also has a samba whistle). Can be replaced by a timbale or a snare drum with the snares turned off. It is normally supported on a shoulder yoke but can be played on a stand.

Surdo A bass drum, played with a felt-headed stick. Can be replaced with an orchestral or kit bass drum.

Tambourin A small tambour, hand held and played with a five-bladed stick to produce a sharp, penetrating rimshot. Any small tambour will do but this part may need supplementing with woodblocks or claves (although these are, strictly speaking, Cuban instruments).

Gonza A two-barrelled shaker (can be replaced by any shaker).

Agogo Twin African bells. A cowbell will suffice, or even a small saucepan.

Two surdo players, with differently-pitched drums (one drum per player), can combine to provide a backing as follows:

The shakers maintain a semiquaver pattern over the surdo pattern.

Then the clave is added:

Other patterns are played over this. At the top of the next page are some typical patterns for the tambourines and agogos, divided into easy, moderate and difficult.

easy

moderate

difficult

Build up the parts bit by bit. Start with the surdos then add the tambourin (this plays the clave rhythm – see page 10, but here it is notated in one bar, i.e. in double time). The other parts can then be fitted around this. Start slowly and build up the speed.

Leave the shakers until last; they can be tiring, especially for beginners, resulting in a loss of rhythmic tightness.

Once the ensemble is working together, try a solo passage for repinique. It is possible to have more than one soloist. The repinique part is often an improvised solo featuring dramatic call-and-response passages. These are usually signalled by the player with the whistle (a two-bar warning: good practice at counting) whereupon the solo passages are answered by the band in unison. Solos tend to last for four bars, after which the band re-enters:

Steel band

Playing in a steel band is a little like playing in a samba band – but with tuned instruments. Few schools are lucky enough to have an authentic band (you will need a specialist tutor to go with it!) but the texture itself can be improvised using tuned percussion and keyboards (some keyboards have quite a good steel drum sound).

The steel band is basically a four-part orchestra. The tune is played by the 'ping pongs', the inner parts by the 'guitars' and 'cellos', and the bass line is played by the 'booms'. Each player has a stick in each hand. The ping pong and boom players use these to play a single line. The guitar and cello players fill out the inner parts each with two notes of the chord, one note per stick.

This texture can be replicated on keyboards in a way that makes it quite accessible to beginners, as the playing technique only needs two fingers.

Here is a typical texture:

* Octaves optional: either one player with two sticks or two players

In up-tempo items it is customary to add a drum kit and some samba-like Latin percussion (see above or Chapter 9).

Steel band arrangements of almost anything are possible using the guidelines above. Making an arrangement of the traditional Caribbean melody below involves working out the underlying harmony. The chords need to be divided between the guitars and cellos and given a catchy rhythm. The bass line will sound better if it, too, has a bit of rhythmic life. Take this well known tune:

An arrangement could be made along these lines:

Tala

This performance is based on the rhythms of **bhangra** (see Chapter 9). The Indian instruments can be substituted as follows:

Dhol   Any two large muted drums played with felt headed sticks, for example congas. A resonant plastic bin will produce a suitably percussive 'thud'.

Tabla   A muted snare drum (strike the skin for the bass tabla and strike the rim with a stick for the more resonant and sharp treble tabla). A pair of bongos will suffice.

Harmonium Keyboard

Bass   Keyboard or any bass instrument

More parts for additional drums, woodblock, shaker and bass can be added.

The aim is to devise subdivisions of the beat, as in the example below. These are patterns that would normally be played by the tabla, and the subdivisions may be articulated by accents or by playing on different parts of the drum. You can play the quavers straight or swung.

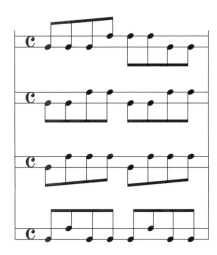

The next stage is to add parts for the dhol:

Lastly a bass line with chordal accompaniment played on the harmonium/keyboard will complete the texture:

Riff ensemble

Chapter 8 included an analysis of Mike Oldfield's *Tubular Bells*. The project below is a riff-based piece of minimalism for any instrument, based on that piece. Provided the harmonic content is kept simple it can be put together in the classroom fairly easily.

First choose a two-chord pattern over two bars (see page 31). Here we will use A minor and G. Devise a simple two-bar riff to go with it. This will form the initial stimulus, which one student (or the teacher) can lead on their own instrument.

Divide the class into families of instruments, according to the resources available: keyboards, tuned and untuned percussion, guitars, strings, woodwind, brass. Keep bass instruments separate.

Start to build, part by part, a backing texture consisting of some chords (possibly a keyboard 'pad'). This backing comprises a two-chord pattern which is an easy one to improvise to.

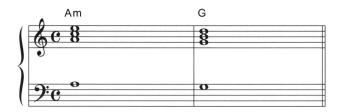

Now start to add the different riffs. These can be as simple or as difficult as the players can handle.

Examples of bass riffs:

Examples of treble riffs:

When the parts are starting to fit together, think about changing the textures, building up and then thinning out.

PART 3
Project Planning

> The remaining four chapters of the book, forming Part 3, are addressed to the teacher, and include guidance on designing activities and worksheets, based on the formats of questions commonly found in exam papers.

CHAPTER 12

Frameworks for Listening

Keeping a listening log

In addition to supporting practical work like performing and composing, listening has a crucial role in most music exams. It is also an opportunity to stimulate discussion.

Students will find it helpful to keep a listening log of the songs they study. This can take the form of a table with two columns: students write down things they notice about the song in their owns words in the left hand column, and the teacher can then go through the list afterwards, adding and explaining the technical vocabulary.

What do you notice	What is it called
Nice tune	Chorus Hook
Lots of singers	Multitracked vocals
Guitar	Lead guitar Distortion Riffs

Focused listening

Listening activities work best when the student is asked to concentrate on a particular element of the music, for example the melody, instrumentation or structure. One approach can be to ask the class (working singly, in pairs, or in small groups) to play the role of an examiner, using a mark sheet to assess the various parts of a song. In the example below, they award an overall mark out of ten, and then select two elements for a mark out of five each. In this way they focus on what they consider to be the strengths of the song. They can also, if this approach is taken, add comments in the shaded section of the chart.

TITLE		
	Comments (optional)	Marks
General impression		$/10$
CHOOSE **TWO** OF THE FOLLOWING:		
Lyrics		$/5$
Backing		$/5$
Structure		$/5$
Melody		$/5$
Rhythm		$/5$
TOTAL marks (for general impression + your two choices):		$/20$

Listening worksheets

Worksheets are usually modelled on exam papers and consist of questions that direct the student to a particular feature or musical element.

Many questions offer multiple choice answers, for example:

Circle two features that are present in this song

middle section   riff   backing vocals   swing rhythm

or:

Circle the letters that correctly match the order of the phrases:

AAAB   AABA   ABBA   ABAB

or, for students who read notation:

Which of these rhythms is the same as the bass drum part?

a)

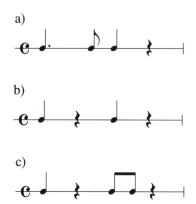

b)

c)

Skeleton scores and chord charts also help the student to focus.

On this 12-bar chord chart, put a cross in the bars where the chord-changes occur:

A question for the more advanced student:

In this four-bar chord pattern (which is repeated throughout the song), identify the chord in the shaded bar:

| D | F | | A |

Alternatively, the student can be asked to write a prose answer. This is suitable for exercises where they are asked to make a simple list of features like the instruments heard (there is an example of this on page 55). The more confident student can be asked to write a short commentary. A good preparation for this is discussion: after listening to a song, it is helpful to consider general questions as well as more detailed analytical ones; for example:

➤ What are some of the features that make a successful pop song?

➤ What is more important – the words or the melody?

➤ How important is the backing?

➤ Does a song need a chorus? If so, why?

➤ Does the length of the song matter? Why?

➤ Are instrumental solos important? At what point in the song might they be best placed?

Comparisons

Comparing one piece of music with another is a popular form of question. On the simplest level the student can be asked, in the form of a multiple choice table such as the one below, to locate particular features. In this example, three contrasting songs are played:

Put a cross in the column of the song where you hear each of the musical features:

	Song 1	Song 2	Song 3
Lead guitar			
Drum machine			
Violin			
Echo effect			
Saxophone			
Drum kit			
Sample			

Other comparisons adopt a 'same-different' format:

What features are the same?	What features are different?

A favourite exam question involves a comparison between two performances of the same piece. Popular music offers a range of opportunities here, as arrangements and 'cover versions' are quite common. Here are some examples:

Dancing in the Street (Martha and the Vandellas / David Bowie and Mick Jagger)
Killing Me Softly with His Song (Roberta Flack / Fugees)
Love is All Around (Wet Wet Wet / Troggs)
American Pie (Don Maclean / Madonna)

Guns'n Roses have covered *Knockin' on Heaven's Door* (Bob Dylan), *Sympathy for the Devil* (Rolling Stones) and *Live and Let Die* (Paul McCartney).

Big Country have a large repertoire of covers including *Summertime* (Gershwin), *Eleanor Rigby* (Beatles) and *Ruby Tuesday* (Rolling Stones).

The boy and girl bands have made many covers:
  Love me for a Reason (Boyzone / The Osmonds)
  When the Going Gets Tough (Boyzone / Billy Ocean)
  Uptown Girl (Westlife / Billy Joel)
  Under the Bridge (All Saints / Red Hot Chilli Peppers).

Two complete CDs of covers are *In My Life* (Beatles songs, collection produced by George Martin) and *Pin Ups* ('60s rock songs covered by David Bowie).

Differentiating worksheets

One of the purposes of worksheets is to monitor student progress so that feedback can be given and strengths and weaknesses identified. It can be helpful, then, if the questions are structured so as to elicit a range of responses. In most examination papers the first question is the least demanding and those that follow become more difficult.

In this example the students are played *Penny Lane* by the Beatles. Questions might be structured as follows:

Question	Answer
Name three instruments that you can hear in this song	Students identify instruments from a multiple choice, e.g. guitar, drums, violin, organ, bass guitar, trumpet.
Name two differences between verse 1 and verse 2	Most students will spot the main differences in instrumentation. The more able will spot the different ending (the second time bar).
Write a short commentary about the structure	Responses will range from the mono-syllabic to structured prose answers. Most will identify the middle section and the trumpet solo. The more able will provide a running order (e.g. A A B A solo B A, etc.) and, if you have covered the topic, the most able will correctly identify 32-bar form.

CHAPTER 13

Designing Worksheets

This chapter includes a range of activities aimed at small groups or pairs, plus ideas for more extended study projects which draw on activities elsewhere in this book.

Worksheets

Worksheets can be prepared using Microsoft Word. The **Draw Table** function will allow you to draw chord charts and question papers. You can also use Sibelius for setting notated questions.

Starting with a stimulus

A short stimulus can provide a creative start to a composition. The ones in the worksheet below are written out but they could just as easily be given aurally. There are five short stimuli: a melodic fragment, a riff, a rhythm, a bass line and a chord progression.

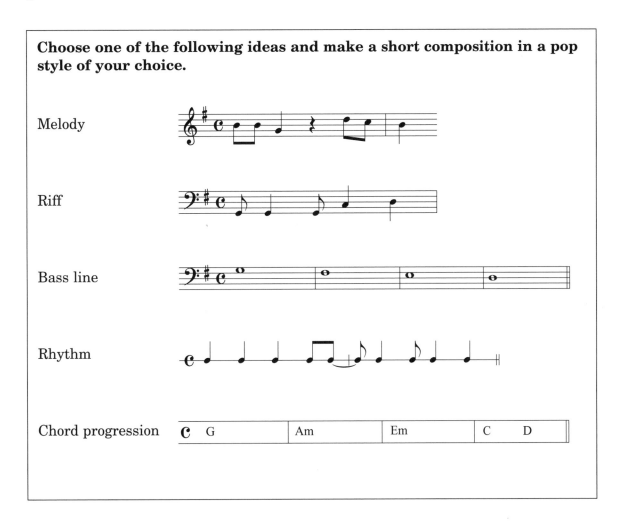

Completions

A completion provides the student with more starting information and clearer guidelines. The chapters on melody, harmony and structure all include ideas for completing phrases, chord progressions and particular forms; the worksheets below show how such tasks might be presented.

Some students may find it easier if the task is very directed – for example by being asked to suggest a missing chord in a given progression.

Complete the chord progression by adding chords in the blank bars.

C	G	Am	Em		C	Dm	

Many of the completions in the chapter on harmony (see page 36) involved chaining progressions together to make a song or section of a song. Some students may find this easier if the choice of chords is limited. In the example below there are opportunities for the more adventurous to modulate, but it still allows for a more basic progression using chords I, IV and V.

Choosing from the chords below, complete the chord chart so as to make a 16-bar verse and an 8-bar middle section.

C   F   G   Am   E   Dm   E♭

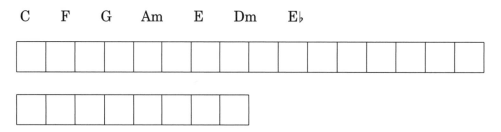

The stronger student can be given fully notated examples to complete:

The bass line below is written out in semibreves. Each bar begins with the root note of the chord. Add another note on the third beat so as to create two minims per bar. Try to maintain a strong melodic bass line.

The following exercise could be undertaken with one student playing the bass line and another adding the treble part.

The 12-bar blues below has been written out with every other two bars of melody left blank. Add suitable melodic phrases in these blank bars.

CHAPTER 14

Schemes of Work

32-bar song

The 32-bar song (see page 47) has been a fundamental form in the history of popular music from Gershwin to Britpop. It can be used to introduce the concept of the middle section as well as being a simple structure within which beginners can learn the basics of harmony.

Prior learning   Work with riffs. Awareness of chords I, IV and V.

Equipment   CD player, keyboards

Introduction   Explain the basic **AABA** structure.

Play examples of 32-bar songs, for instance:
Ol' Man River (by Jerome Kern)
Everyday (Buddy Holly)
Yesterday (the Beatles) (with 7-bar **A** sections)
All Right (Supergrass)

Using listening logs and chord charts, identify **A** and **B** sections.

Development   Analyse one of the songs.

Compile a simple chord chart for an eight-bar section.

Add a middle eight.

Play the chords and add a bass line.

Performance   Play the song to the class.

The instruments of popular music

Prior learning None – this is an introductory scheme of work.

Introduction The three songs below might be regarded as milestones in the development of instruments and technology. They are separated by gaps of seventeen years.

Apache (the Shadows, 1960)

The Shadows were Cliff Richard's backing band and helped to establish the classic four-piece guitar line-up of lead, rhythm and bass guitars and drums. The lead guitarist, Hank Marvin, developed a clear tone that stood out from the backing, and he used many effects like the tremolo arm (a lever attached to the bridge which allows the player to raise and lower the tuning) and echo. Nowadays echo effects are created digitally, but Hank Marvin used an echo unit which employed a tape loop with multiple replay heads.

Showroom Dummies (Kraftwerk, 1977)

Kraftwerk are a German band that pioneered the use of synthesisers that led to the '80s style of **electro rock**. The drum track is provided by a drum machine which, in this example, has a very mechanical feel. All the other instrumental parts are performed on synthesisers.

No Good (Start the Dance) (the Prodigy, 1994)

This is an example of techno, with driving rhythms and heavy guitar riffs. The Prodigy were not the first club act to employ samplers (see page *), but they were among the first to achieve major chart success. What makes this song interesting is the inclusion of another club hit (Kelly Charles' *No Good For Me*), sampled and woven into the song – a device adopted by many later artists, including Eminem. The song consists of a collage of samples – including the drum patterns – looped on a computer to form tracks. Note the distorted flute part.

Development Each of these songs might lead to a more detailed study of instrumentation:

The Shadows: guitar bands (the Beatles, Stone Roses, Franz Ferdinand), heavy rock virtuosi (Jimi Hendrix, Van Halen, Led Zeppelin)

Kraftwerk: Electro rock (Ultravox, Human League), Synth-based acts (Pet Shop Boys)

Prodigy: Club music (Fatboy Slim)

Practical work Bring favourite songs to school to play. What are the instruments?

Do the listening exercise on page 55.

Songs with a message

Prior learning   The introductory work involves listening and discussing. Students will need some background in group work and songwriting to complete the project at the end.

Love songs   A comparison between love songs by men and women:

Three songs by women:
Can't Get You Out of my Head (Kylie Minogue)
Nothing Compares to U (Sinead O'Connor)
I Will Survive (Gloria Gaynor)

Three songs by men:
I'm not in Love (10CC)
Wonderwall (Oasis)
Dry Your Eyes (the Streets)

Questions:
How do the different songwriters approach the idea of love?
Do the women and men songwriters approach it differently?
How is the idea of love depicted in the *music*?

Political songs   Political pop has a long history. The folk singer Woody Guthrie (e.g. *This Land is Your Land*) was blacklisted by the US government in the 1950s for his political views on civil rights, and influenced a generation of singers of whom Bob Dylan is best known. Dylan took a stand against nuclear weapons when the Cold War was at its height in the 1960s (*Hard Rain's A-Gonna Fall*, *Masters of War*). John Lennon took a similar anti-war stand against the Vietnam War (*Give Peace a Chance*, *Happy Christmas War is Over*) as did Jimmy Cliff (*Vietnam*). Youth unemployment and the government of Margaret Thatcher became a target for the punk movement (*White Riot* by the Clash and *Anarchy in the UK* by the Sex Pistols). Many of the songs of Bob Marley (see pages 97–98) have a strong political message about black liberation and world peace (*Exodus*, *One Love*, *Get Up Stand Up*, *Redemption Song*). His involvement in Jamaican politics led to an attempt on his life, and he was forced for a while to live in exile.

Questions:

What political issues are addressed?

Many of the songs have angry lyrics. How is this anger expressed in the music?

Practical   Compose a song. For a love song choose a point of view (e.g. lost love) and for a political song choose an issue.

Cut and paste

Cutting and pasting is the basic technique of much contemporary popular music. This scheme of work can be focused on the computer or it can be undertaken with live instruments. This scheme of work would serve as an introduction to the techniques of club music.

Prior learning Basic computer sequencing skills. Group-work composing skills.

Introduction Play examples of dub reggae (see page 106).

Practical Compile a simple dub reggae piece using two-bar patterns (see page 31).

Development Play examples of club music, for example Fatboy Slim (page 53) and Basement Jaxx (page 123).

Questions:
Do all the tracks play all the time?
In what order do the tracks enter?
What is the structure of the songs?

Composing Compose a piece based on short ideas, repeating them to create different tracks and interesting textures. This can be done on the computer, but if the composition is for live instruments the student may find it helpful to arrange the tracks on a track diagram – similar to a track display on a computer screen (see page 118).

Rhythm

Prior learning None – this is an introductory scheme of work.

Introduction What makes pop rhythm different? Play and discuss pop and jazz arrangements of classical pieces, for example Duke Ellington's *Peer Gynt* and *Nutcracker* suites, comparing them with the originals (see page 8).

Practical Do some of the warm-up exercises included in the chapter on rhythm (page 7), concentrating on the exercise based on the *clave* pattern in order to learn the concept of syncopation.

Development Working in groups, write a simple riff-based piece (see page 80).

Study rhythms of the world, for example Latino (page 107) and bhangra (page 110).

Performance Create a performance of a samba piece for the whole class (see page 128).

The voice

This scheme of work is intended to develop ideas for composing for the voice, rather than being a history of the voice in popular music.

Introduction   Play and discuss two contrasting examples:

Dry Your Eyes (the Streets) – a spoken verse and a very simple sung chorus.

The Great Gig in the Sky (Pink Floyd) – a short spoken introduction followed by a wordless and gymnastic solo from session singer Clare Torry.

Questions:

Is it necessary to sing? Can the spoken word be just as effective?

How can the composer adapt to a singer who does not have a big vocal range? Examples: the Beatles writing for Ringo Starr (*With a Little Help from my Friends* and *Yellow Submarine* both have very few notes), and songs written for Kylie Minogue and Madonna, which also tend to be quite restricted in range.

Practical   Working in groups, do the songwriting project on page 25. This is based on Madonna's *Like a Prayer* and involves writing a simple six-note melody.

Extension   Listen to raps, for example:
The Real Slim Shady and *Stan* (Eminen) – see page 120
Give it Away (Red Hot Chilli Peppers)

Working in groups or pairs, compose a rap – see page 82.

See if you can add a sung vocal part to the rap – for example a chorus.

CHAPTER 15

The Computer in the Classroom

The computer is often shut away in a side room of the music department or set up as a series of workstations for the students to use singly or in pairs. This chapter includes ideas for streamlining its use and also extending it as a useful tool in classroom teaching, especially for listening and performing.

Listening

The advantage of a computer over a CD player is that the sounds can be changed quickly. Entry-level programs like Dance eJay and Music Maker offer numerous opportunities for devising listening exercises because the material can be assembled very easily. The computer sound card can be connected to the classroom hi-fi (from the output of the sound card to the auxiliary input of the amplifier) and this will give a better quality of sound than the computer's own multimedia speakers. Take care with the output level from the computer.

The comparison type of listening exercise (see page 137) can be accomplished by arranging two or more versions of the same song. These can be saved separately although it will be quicker to use in the classroom if they follow one another *segue*. This will allow you to see all the versions on screen at once: you can also start and stop the computer at will and repeat sections. Preparation involves using sampled material to compile a short dance piece, then devising one or two remixes. Obvious things to change will be the drum patterns and inner parts, or adding or subtracting solo material. It is also possible to vary the structure by, for example, arranging several versions with the sections in a different order.

These activities can also be undertaken in conjunction with a worksheet.

Questions might take the following forms:

> There are three sections (**ABC**), some of which are repeated. Write down the order in which you hear them (e.g. **ABBCA**).

> Which of the sections is different in the remixed version – **A**, **B** or **C**?
> Name two differences.
> Name two similarities.

Alternatively the students could be given multiple choice questions about the remixes, for example:

> Which of the following represents the order of the sections?

> **AABCAB**   **AACBBA**   **AABCBA**

More detailed work is possible with a MIDI program. The **drum editor** (see page 16) will allow you to play several versions of a drum pattern, each with a subtle difference. For example three different hi-hat patterns could be played and the student asked to put them in order. You may have to reduce the speed in the case of a complex pattern; this, too, is easy with a MIDI sequencing program.

Similar variations can be created for the bass drum pattern, or for a bass or keyboard riff. More elaborate MIDI arrangements can be created for teaching harmony.

In the following example a skeleton chord chart is given to the students showing a four-chord pattern with one chord missing.

The computer then plays three versions of the above pattern – a simple arrangement for keyboard, bass and drums – each repeated several times and each with a different chord in the blank bar which the student has to identify:

Performing

The computer can also be used – karaoke style – to provide a backing band. This is especially useful for teaching melody writing and improvisation. Here, amplification is essential and so is balance. You may have to experiment a bit before performers can hear the backing as well as themselves, but it shouldn't present any more difficulties than trying to lead the lesson from, say, a piano.

As with listening, the entry-level programs work well, although you may find they are a little limited in style. Programs like Dance eJay are based on samples, often two- or four-bar looped chordal patterns, typically based in A minor, which can be selected and manipulated to make a backing. A set of percussion tracks can provide a useful backing for a live percussion session, acting as a rhythmic anchor and usually more interesting than the drum patterns available on a drum machine.

A MIDI performance consisting of a simple bass line or chord pattern on a keyboard can provide support for a soloist – and the programs will allow you to slow down or transpose the performance to suit the player. Patterns consisting of two chords are easiest – along the lines of the main theme of Dave Brubeck's *Take Five*. Page 31 includes ideas for two-chord patterns.

Beginners may find it easier to experiment with improvised melody if they are limited to a few notes or specific figurations or rhythms. The examples below (and on the next page) are for an exercise in D minor:

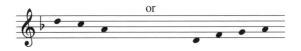

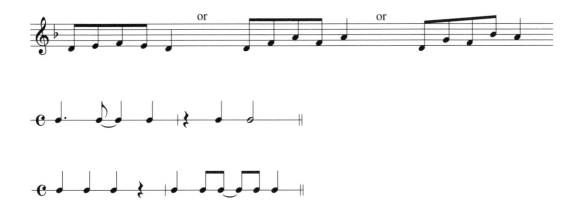

Another strategy is to set up a call-and-response backing. Here the computer plays an arrangement with built-in silences that are completed by the player or players:

Composing

Compiling a library of exercises and projects and loading them onto the computer at the start of the lesson can save a lot of time. For example, a CD of frequently used samples and MIDI files of backing tracks can be loaded easily and quickly.

In most composing activities students will be working alone or in pairs, and most of the ideas for worksheets involving completions (see page 140) could equally be accomplished live at the computer.

Completions

Here are some examples of completion tasks:

The teacher records a four- or eight-bar chord pattern as a backing track. This consists of a lead melodic line, a chordal rhythm part, bass and drums. This is then saved in four different versions – in each version one of the four parts is missing. The student is given one of these versions and asked to complete the missing part, for example 'add a bass line to this four-bar arrangement'. You may have to create an empty track on which you have already selected the instrument to be added. Then all the student has to do is select that track and play and record (or enter) their part. The part to be completed can be identified on the track display and the student can select tracks to listen to by muting and soloing.

Saxophone				
Keyboard				
to complete (Bass)				
Drums				

The teacher records a solo melody or bass line. This is saved in several versions – in each version a portion is omitted (one or two bars). The student has to complete the missing portions. To make this easier, create a second empty track below as a working track on which the student's added portions will be recorded – otherwise, if they work on the original track they will not be able to delete mistakes easily without deleting the 'question'.

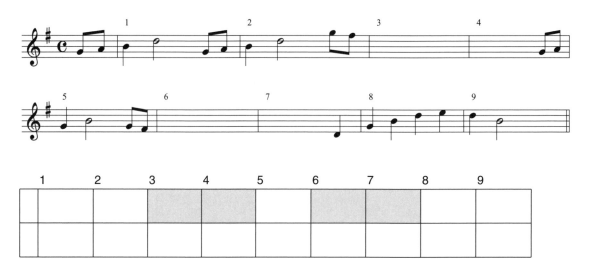

A more difficult version of the above task involves making an arrangement of a standard form, such as a 12-bar blues or 32-bar song (see Chapter 4), and including gaps for completion along the lines of the 12-bar blues worksheet on page 141. Similarly, the student could be asked to complete the middle eight (or part of the middle eight) in a 32-bar song. Here, they will have to be shown how to move the locators so they can isolate and record a section.

Stimuli

The stimuli in the exercise on page 139 can be saved on the computer as a single track to form the basis of a composition. However, it will help if each stimulus is 'rounded up' to the nearest bar so it can be copied easily. For added interest the stimulus could be drawn from a sample library. Samples will have to be matched to the tempo of the computer so they loop neatly (see page 119).

Glossary

A cappella Sung without an instrumental accompaniment

Al fine To the end

Ambience The natural acoustic of a performing space

Arabesque A melodic decoration

Arpeggio Melodic figurations based on a broken chord

Backing track The recorded accompaniment of a song without the vocals

Binary form A piece in two halves, both usually repeated and with a *cadence* in the middle

Blank verse Poetry without a rhyming, metrical structure

BPM Beats per minute

Bridge This term has a flexible use: sometimes it refers to a short passage linking the end of a verse to the chorus (also called a **pre-chorus**) and sometimes it is used as an alternative term for a *middle section*

Broken chords Chords in which the notes are played one after the other instead of at the same time

Cadence A point in a musical phrase where the harmony comes to rest, e.g. on the tonic chord (a perfect cadence) or on the dominant (an imperfect cadence)

Call-and-response An alternation between the soloist and the chorus (or band).

Canon A melody which combines with itself, the second part entering later

Chamber music Classical music for a small ensemble, intended for performance in a room rather than a concert hall

Chorus The memorable section of a song in which the words are the same each time

Click track A recorded metronome pulse to help the performers keep in time

Close harmony A vocal arrangement in which the notes of the chord are close together, rather than spread over a wide range

Coda A short ending section

Consecutive fifths Melodic parts which move in parallel, a perfect fifth apart

Contrary motion Melodic parts which move in opposite directions

Counterpoint The combination of two or more melodic parts

Cover version An arrangement of a popular song

Cycle of fifths A chord progression in which the roots of the chords move up or down in a sequence of perfect fifths

Da capo (also written DC) Return to the beginning

DI Direct injection – when an instrument is connected directly to the mixing desk (sometimes through a DI box which matches the output of the instrument to the desk)

Envelope The 'shape' of a sound, i.e. its beginning (attack) and its dying away (decay)

Falsetto   The upper, treble part of a male voice
Four-part harmony   Chord progressions consisting of four parts

Glissando   A fast run or slide between two notes
Grace note   A note added to decorate a melody

Heterophony   Two versions of a melody played at the same time
Homophonic   All the parts played in the same rhythm

Import   To introduce data from one computer program into another
Interface   A computer connection
Inversion   A chord in which a note other the root is in the bass

Jazz standard   A well known jazz song

Lead sheet   A score in which only the vocal line, words and chord symbols are given
Loop   To repeat. A **drum loop** is a sampled pattern intended to be copied and
    repeated
Low tech   A deliberate attempt to create an unrefined recorded sound, usually for a
    'retro' effect

Metre   The division of a pulse into beats and bars
Middle   A contrasting section in a song, usually with a change of harmony or key,
    often eight bars long, hence *middle eight*
MIDI file   A means of storing MIDI data
Minimalism   A style of music consisting of repeated phrases and patterns which
    gradually change
Mix down   The act of combining all the tracks of a recording to make a final version
Mode   Each mode is a scale with a particular sequence of tones and semitones. The
    modes are usually thought of in terms of the white notes of the piano: for example,
    the Mixolyidian mode uses the white notes from G to G, the Aeolian (or 'minor')
    mode runs from A to A.
Modulation   A process in which the key of a song changes from one key to another.
    In a **passing modulation** it occurs briefly as part of a phrase. A **tertiary
    modulation** is one in which the key moves up or down by a third.
Motif   A short musical idea

Non-essential note   A note, usually in the melody, which is not part of the
    underlying chord

Ornament   A short decorative pattern added to a melody
Ostinato   A short phrase which is repeated many times
Outboard   A special effect which is plugged into an instrument, usually a guitar
Overdub   To build up parts or tracks in a recording, one by one

Passing note   A melody note, not part of the chord but lying between two notes
    which are
Pedal   A bass note which stays the same while the chord changes above it
Pentatonic   Based on a five-note scale, for example the black notes of the piano
Polyphony   The combination of two or more parts
Pre-chorus   See **Bridge**

Recitative and aria An operatic form consisting of an introduction in which the singer delivers the text as a recitation, accompanied only by a few chords, followed by an aria with a flowing melody

Refrain A chorus

Relative minor/major Every major key has a relative minor, whose root is to be found by counting down the scale by three notes, and which takes its notes from that major scale

Romantic miniature A short piece, usually for solo instrumentalist, made popular in the early 1800s

Rondo A form in which a theme keeps returning with contrasting sections in between

Scat A style of jazz singing based on wordless syllables

Segue To follow without a break

Sequencing The art of compiling instrumental performances using MIDI

Skeleton score A score with only the bare details included

Soloing (tracks) Selecting a single track to listen to on a recording device

Song sheet A score which includes the vocal line and words plus a simplified version of the backing arranged for keyboard or guitar

Species counterpoint A system for teaching sixteenth-century *counterpoint* starting with regular note values and building to parts with more complex rhythms

Stepwise movement A melody in which the notes move one degree of the scale at a time, rather than in leaps

Strophic A song which consists only of repeated verses

Syncopation A rhythm with accents and/or note values which are not on the metrical beat

Ternary form A form based on an ABA structure

Transpose To play in a different key

Unplugged Played using acoustic instruments

Verse A section of a song which is repeated with the same melody but different words

Voicing The choice of which note is played or sung at the top of a chord, and where the other notes are placed

Walking bass A bass line played in steady (usually crotchet) note values

Word painting A classical device in which the meaning of the words is illustrated by the music

Index of Artists
with song and album titles

Classical composers and their works are included in the General Index (page 158).

General Index